Implementing Successful
Post-Acquisition Management

Pearson Education

In an increasingly competitive world, it is quality of thinking that gives an edge – an idea that opens new doors, a technique that solves a problem, or an insight that simply helps make sense of it all.

We work with leading authors in the fields of management and finance to bring cutting-edge thinking and best learning practice to a global market.

Under a range of leading imprints, including *Financial Times Prentice Hall*, we create world-class print publications and electronic products giving readers knowledge and understanding which can be applied, whether studying or at work.

To find out more about our business and professional products, you can visit us at www.business-minds.com.

For other Pearson Education publications, visit www.pearsoned-ema.com.

MANAGEMENT BRIEFINGS
EXECUTIVE BRIEFING

Implementing Successful Post-Acquisition Management

DUNCAN ANGWIN

FINANCIAL TIMES
Prentice Hall

London   New York   San Francisco   Toronto   Sydney
Tokyo   Singapore   Hong Kong   Cape Town   Madrid
Paris   Milan   Munich   Amsterdam

PEARSON EDUCATION LIMITED

Head Office:
Edinburgh Gate
Harlow CM20 2JE
Tel: +44 (0)1279 623623
Fax: +44 (0)1279 431059

London Office:
128 Long Acre, London WC2E 9AN
Tel: +44 (0)207 447 2000
Fax: +44 (0)207 240 5771
Website: www.business-minds.com

First published in Great Britain in 2000

ISBN 0 273 64225 1

British Library Cataloguing in Publication Data
A CIP catalogue record for this book can be obtained from the British Library.

10 9 8 7 6 5 4 3 2 1

Typeset by Boyd Elliott Typesetting
Printed and bound in Great Britain

The Publishers' policy is to use paper manufactured from sustainable forests.

About the author

Dr Duncan Angwin has the unusual distinction of having spent half his time transacting acquisitions and half his time studying them. He spent eight years in the City working on domestic and cross-border acquisitions as well as carrying out corporate advisory work for leading merchant banks such as Hambros Bank and Banque Paribas. His curiosity as to the limitations of the acquisition process, such as why apparently good deals from a banker's perspective may turn out as poor acquisitions, led him to engage in full-time research on managing acquisitions. A PhD in post-acquisition management later, he now consults and lectures widely on the subject.

Dr Angwin holds a position as lecturer in Strategic Management at Warwick Business School, University of Warwick. He has published widely on mergers and acquisitions and appeared often in the media. He consults as sole practitioner and as associate consultant for several specialist integration consultancies. He also lectures regularly to corporate audiences and leading business schools throughout Europe.

Dr Angwin is a PhD from Warwick University. He also holds an MBA from Cranfield University, an M.Phil and M.A. (Hons) from Cambridge University.

Dr Duncan Angwin can be contacted at:

Marketing and Strategic Management Group
Warwick Business School
University of Warwick
Coventry CV4 7AL
England

Tel: (direct) +44. (0) 1203.524541
or
Tel: (direct) +44. (0) 1865.514898
Tel: (office) +44. (0) 1203.523914

E-mail: Duncan.Angwin@warwick.ac.uk

To Kay,
Christopher, Katherine, William
for
inspiration and sympathy

Contents

Preface

Accquistions are a double-edged sword. They can be most effective in achieving corporate strategic renewal with the potential to reorientate and restructure the acquirer as well as build its base of capabilities. They can also result in significant value destruction through costly implementation and indeed cause substantial damage to both the acquired and acquiring companies.

This book focuses upon the post-acquisition phase where the battle for value is won or lost. We show that there is not just one best way to manage a firm once it has been acquired but that there are several approaches, each of which can be effective in different circumstances. Although the book focuses upon the post-acquisition phase, we emphasise throughout, the importance of the entire acquisition process as well as its role in the acquirer's overall strategy.

It is important to establish how this book views acquisitions. Most of the sources available on merger and acquisition activity show vast numbers of acquisitions taking place. However, these aggregate figures contain a myriad different types of deals. In particular, substantial numbers of acquisitions reported are MBOs/MBIs, asset purchases, financial restructurings, partial acquisitions, subsidiary acquisitions, to name but a few. These types of acquisition generally exhibit reduced levels of post-acquisition management complexity and will not be covered in this book.

The handling of the term 'merger' is also important. In American books, mergers are taken to mean both acquisitions and mergers. In this book the terms will be kept distinct as there can be differences between mergers and acquisitions in the way the combined companies are managed post-deal. However, it is worth remembering that, despite the recent pronounced rise in the number of mega-mergers, in many instances they are described in hindsight as acquisitions without premiums. This is often a reflection of specific integration difficulties associated with mergers, which require the parties to resort to behaviour more characteristic of acquisitions to resolve. Whilst no premium is attractive in giving greater financial room for manoeuvre, mergers often come with hidden integration costs.

This book then is concerned with the complete acquisition of stand-alone companies, which allows the full range of post-acquisition potentialities and difficulties to be demonstrated.

Acknowledgements

The author wishes to thank all those senior acquisition managers who so generously shared their experiences of living through the post-acquisition process. These interviews form the basis of groundbreaking research. In particular I would like to thank Lars Berntson, Paul Halliday, Peter Jackson of USF, Ronald Moss, and David Willis of Level (3) Communications. Many other interviewees were vital to the research but in order to protect their identities and their businesses, all information relating to their acquisitions has been anonymised.

Many other advisors and observers have contributed directly to this book and indirectly through sponsoring related research. In particular the author would like to thank Andrew Collinson, Tony Green, Steve Baker and David Brown of Collinson Grant Consultants, John Dunford and Eric Benedict of Ernst and Young, Garnet Twigg, John Ibbotson and Gerard Gray of London Consulting, Brett Saville of PricewaterhouseCoopers. In academia, the author is grateful for the many discussions and insights from Professor John McGee, Professor Robin Wensley and Dr Terry McNulty of Warwick Business School, University of Warwick; Dr Richard Whittington, Dr David Faulkner and Dr Laura Empson of Said School of Business, University of Oxford; and Professor Peter Grinyer of Aberdeen University. The author would also like to acknowledge the many Executives and MBAs of Warwick Business School for their lively discussions and support.

The publisher and author would like to thank the following for their kind permissions to reproduce text and articles:

Butterworth Heinemann for Figure 4.18 Amount of restraint upon individuals and culture type, reproduced from Cartwright and Cooper (1992: 75) *Mergers and Acquisitions – the Human Factor* and Figure 4.19 Types of organisational and individual acculturation, with potential outcomes, reproduced from Cartwright and Cooper (1992: 79) *Mergers and Acquisitions – the Human Factor*.

Elsevier Science for Figure 1.1 Cross-border acquisitions compared to domestic acquisitions, reproduced from Angwin and Savill (1997: 15, 4: 423) 'Strategic Perspectives on European Cross-Border Acquisitions', *European Management Journal*.

Heist for Table 6.2 Issues for consideration amongst higher education mergers, from Palfreyman, Thomas and Warner (1998) *How to Manage a Merger . . . or Avoid One*.

Pearson Education Ltd and Prentice Hall Europe for Figure 4.15 The cultural web, Figure 4.16 Questions to surface real culture and Figure 4.20 Force field analysis, all from Johnson and Scholes (1999: 74, 82, 86) *Exploring Corporate Strategy*, 5th edition.

Pitman Publishing/Pearson Education Ltd for Figure 4.5 The critical path for some human resource integration issues, adapted from Slack, Chambers, Harland, Harrison, Johnston (1998) *Operations Management* 2nd edition.

Times Newspapers Limited for the extract on page 64, from Durman (1998 April 23) 'Leschly blames Glaxo for failed merger.'

The Economist for use of various quotations throughout the book.

The author and publisher have made every effort to seek permission for quotations used in this book.

'Strategy is all very well, but it is nothing without implementation'

(*FT*, 21 August 1997)

'Plenty of people have great ideas: the hard bit is implementing them'

Charles Allen, CEO Granada Group (cited in the *FT*, 21 August 1997)

Introduction

Mergers and acquisitions are again dominating the headlines of the financial press. 1998 saw some $2.4 trillion of deals, an increase of 50 per cent on the previous year. In particular there has been a spate of mega-mergers to create global giants. The end of 1998 saw Travellers/Citicorp merging to form the world's biggest financial services group and Exxon and Mobil announcing an $80bn merger. 1999 has continued the trend for mega-deals with a hostile bid from AT&T for MediaOne for $58bn and the intention at least to create Europe's first supranational with the proposed merger between Deutsche Telekom and Telecom Italia in an $162bn deal.

During this sustained record-breaking wave of merger and acquisition activity, most attention has focused upon 'doing the deal' with continued press speculation about the size of the next mega-deal. However, the important question is how these new mergers and acquisitions will be managed. Will it be a case of act in haste and repent at leisure? Will those deals match up to shareholder expectations, will market share be enhanced, will employee morale be sustained, will value be created?

All these questions and more will depend upon the way in which the post-merger/acquisition process is handled. Indeed, the weight of evidence suggests that some 50–60 per cent of all acquisitions fail and this can be largely attributed to the quality of post-acquisition management. Managing the post-acquisition phase then is critical for success.

This book sets out to show that there are several quite different ways of handling the post-acquisition phase. Some strategies are about minimising risk and create little value for the acquirer. Others aim to create high levels of value but also entail very significant risks to both acquiring and acquired companies. We suggest that there is no one right post-acquisition style, as different styles are appropriate in different contexts. However, we do believe that a consistent approach in a clearly defined style which runs throughout the entire acquisition process is most likely to result in a successful outcome.

Why focus on the post-acquisition phase?

THE CONTEXT: RECORD LEVELS OF ACQUISITION ACTIVITY

The latest figures show that 1998 continued the record-breaking wave of acquisition activity in the UK and US. The acquisition of UK public companies reached its highest level since records began, with 2,278 transactions valued at £90.1bn (*Acquisitions Monthly*, 20 January 1999).

Whilst Europe struggles towards a level playing field, the drive towards a single market has encouraged internal, cross-border acquisitions. Free of the political barriers that have fragmented their markets, many European companies have sought to consolidate their efforts as a means of matching the advantages in economic scale of their US and Far East counterparts (Calori and Lubatkin, 1994). At the same time, the initial fears of Fortress Europe as well as its size and sophistication have made it an attractive hunting ground for non-European multi-nationals.

Such factors have led to cross-border acquisitions becoming an increasingly important feature of European business activity. In the ten years to 1995, the value[1] of cross-border acquisitions rose tenfold from £2bn to some £20bn and the number of deals increased fivefold to 655. Despite the boom in take-overs in the late 1980s and early 1990s, Figure 1.1 shows that European cross-border deals have been gaining steadily in significance over that ten year period from 15 to 30 per cent of the total.

Fig. 1.1 Cross-border acquisitions compared to domestic acquisitions (Bid numbers)

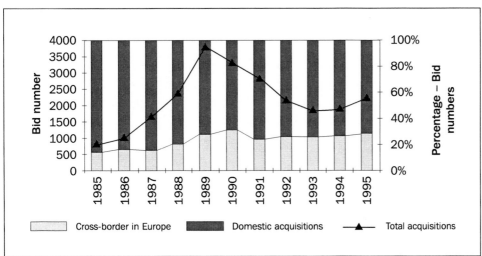

Source: Angwin and Savill (1997: 423) Reprinted from European Management Journal, 15, Angwin and Savill, 'Strategic Perspectives on European Cross-Border Acquisitions', 423–435, 1997, with permission from Elsevier Science

Recent data suggests that cross-border activity continues to surge forward with activity in Western Europe totalling $229.6bn (KPMG, 1998), an increase of 60 per cent on the previous year, and already in the first quarter of 1999,

European-wide deals[2] have amounted to some \$350bn (Thomson Financial Securities Data, 1999). Although this figure has been inflated by the Telecom Italia deal, there were also a record number of deals.

LARGE NUMBERS OF ACQUISITIONS FAIL

With so much acquisition activity taking place, one would expect there to be substantial evidence that acquisitions are largely successful. However, it would seem that success is achieved in signing the deal, rather than in post-acquisition performance.

Domestic acquisition failure rates

Numerous surveys of acquisition performance suggest that around 45–60 per cent of deals fail. For UK/UK deals, Kitching (1974) stated that 47 per cent of acquisitions failed or were not worth making. Hunt of LBS/Egon Zehnder (Hunt et al, 1986) focused upon surviving managers' perceptions of the acquisition, in both the acquiring and acquired companies, some years after the deal and found that 47 per cent felt the acquisition had failed to live up to expectations. Hunt (1990) examined managerial perceptions, accountancy data and stock market share movements, and recorded a failure rate of 50 per cent. Consultancies have generally reported slightly higher rates of failure (*see* Table 1.1).

Table 1.1 Consultancy and business press evidence on acquisition failure

Consultancy	Date	Method	Failure rate %
Business International	1973	400 postal questionnaires	49
	1978	150 postal questionnaires	48–56
Coopers and Lybrand	1992	Qualitative in-depth interviews with senior executives in the UK's top 100 companies	54
Coopers and Lybrand	1996	125 companies. Low revenues, cash flow, profitability	66
A.T. Kearney	1997	115 multi-billion mergers 1993–6. Those not creating 'substantial returns for shareholders' (dividends and share appreciation)	58
Mercer MC	1995	150 companies. Poor returns to shareholders after three years	50
Mercer MC	1997	300 companies. Below average (for industry sector) returns to shareholders	57
McKinsey	1995	Examined 58 acquisitions. Success was measured as financial return exceeding the cost of capital	58.6

Cross-border acquisition failure rates

Failure rates amongst cross-border acquisitions appear to be an area of some dispute. In their survey of 142 top executives of leading acquirers in major European countries, Angwin and Savill (1997) have shown that there is a general perception amongst European top executives that cross-border acquisitions are riskier than domestic ones. Top managers cite increased complexity in areas such as cultural differences and geographical distance as reasons why cross-border deals are less successful than domestic ones. The little evidence that is available on cross-border acquisition performance, however, suggests that this may not be the case. Kitching (1974) interviewed the top executives of 407 acquisitions in Europe and found that Europeans achieved a 54 per cent success rate. Consultants Bleeke and Ernst of McKinsey (1993: 80) reported a success rate of 57 per cent, 'much higher than anticipated'. We believe that an explanation for these counter-intuitive results lies in the differences in post-acquisition choices open to domestic and cross-border acquisitions. Reduced possibilities for integration may also serve to reduce the risk of failure.

PRE-ACQUISITION FACTORS ARE POOR PREDICTORS OF POST-ACQUISITION PERFORMANCE

The immediate reaction of many executives when they realise that an acquisition has failed is to retreat into pre-acquisition explanations: *'We paid too much'*. *'We should have planned it better'*. *'We shouldn't have diversified but acquired a similar business'*. A great deal of time and effort has been put into identifying pre-acquisition factors as predictors of success. The main factors associated with positive performance, for which there is empirical evidence, are examined below.

Ratio of acquired firm sales to acquiring firm

Where acquired firm sales are less than 2 per cent of acquiring firm sales, 84 per cent of such acquisitions fail (Kitching, 1974). At the other end of the spectrum from catching minnows, larger acquisitions increase the risk to performance and can be a case of *'biting off more than you can chew from both a managerial and financial viewpoint'* (Kusewitt, 1985: 159).

Acquisition rate

In a study of 138 very acquisitive companies,[3] Kusewitt (1985) found a negative relationship between acquisition rate and performance[4] where more than one acquisition was made per year. It would seem that: '"corporate indigestion" stemming from "acquisition fever" is a very real threat to the success of an acquisition programme' (Kusewitt, 1985: 159). The stock market also seems aware of this issue as there is some evidence that analysts mark down the performance of acquisitions made too soon to one another (Hayward, 1999).

Pre-acquisition financial health of the acquired company

Where the acquired company has poor pre-acquisition financial health, 42.8 per cent of acquisitions failed and a further 19.1 per cent were perceived as not worth doing (Kitching, 1974). Buying financially weak companies in the hope of achieving a turnaround appears to involve high risk, which is not adequate compensation for their cheapness.[5] More successful acquisitions tend to be of highly profitable companies (Kusewitt, 1985).

Related versus unrelated acquisitions

There is a lot of debate on the issue of whether related acquisitions are likely to be more successful than unrelated ones. Managers believe intuitively that acquiring related businesses will be more successful. However, empirical studies show the issue to be unclear. For instance, substantial studies by Kitching (1974), Singh and Montgomery (1987) and Shelton (1988) state that higher returns accrue in related acquisitions. However, Lubatkin (1983) concludes that related mergers do not create more value than unrelated ones and Chatterjee (1986) and Anslinger and Copeland (1996) find that unrelated mergers perform better than related ones.

The basis for managers expecting related acquisitions to result in more successful outcomes is that there should be synergies which can create value. However, whilst this suggests potential, realising synergies is both risky and difficult. In addition, there can be ambiguity in the way in which relatedness is viewed; often being considered in purely product and market terms. This can conceal significant differences between organisations and lead to unfounded assumptions about the ease of achieving synergies.

Acquisition experience

There is some evidence that the acquirer's experience plays an important role in overall acquisition performance. However, this relationship is complex. We cannot say that greater acquisition experience will necessarily result in better acquisitions. We can say though that experience is useful for judging each acquisition differently from previous ones, so that learning from earlier activities is learning when *not* to apply previous lessons (Shanley, 1994). A recent study of 241 acquisitions in the US, 1985–95, shows that experience of a number of prior small mistakes in acquisition management is likely to result in better performance from the current acquisition (Hayward, 1999). Experience in terms of number of previous minor errors and their diversity can, therefore, help acquirers to appreciate what is special about the current acquisition. In addition, other research takes the view that experience is only important under specific conditions, such as making hostile bids for unhealthy companies (Hunt, 1990).

Pre-acquisition planning

Another influential factor is pre-acquisition planning. However, the emphasis in planning appears to be on trying to avoid disruption rather than on realising the synergies needed for economic performance.

Why looking at pre-acquisition factors isn't enough

The difficulty with pre-acquisition factors as predictors of post-acquisition outcomes is that they assume a direct link with success and post-acquisition change. Whilst pre-acquisition factors do predict some changes in the post-acquisition phase, much of the variation in post-acquisition change is not explained. Yet, post-acquisition changes are significant predictors of post-acquisition performance. In other words, concentrating upon pre-acquisition factors tends to ignore the distorting effect of the post-acquisition phase. At best, pre-acquisition factors are only loosely linked with post-acquisition change (Shanley, 1994: 407)

Angwin and Wensley/Ernst and Young (1995) have given a practical insight to this difficulty with their in-depth interviewing of a wide range of top executives. Whilst different perceptions of aspects of the acquisition process were evident, based upon executive responsibilities, there was a clear agreement about the disconnectedness between pre- and post-acquisition phases.

POST-ACQUISITION MANAGEMENT IS THE KEY TO MAKING ACQUISITIONS WORK, BUT IT IS POORLY UNDERSTOOD

The key to making acquisitions work is the way in which the post-acquisition phase is managed. Too often top management, investors and the media concentrate upon doing the deal and ignore the aftermath. In the words of *The Economist* (4 January 1997):

> *Why do so many mergers miss the mark?: what seems to link most mergers that fail is the acquirer's obsession with the deal itself, coupled with too little attention to what happens next.*

Planning for the post-acquisition phase will undoubtedly help the overall acquisition process. A survey by Coopers and Lybrand (1992) asked respondents for the main causes of acquisition failure. 80 per cent stated that inadequate planning for post-acquisition management was a cause of failure. When respondents were asked for the main reason for success, 76 per cent cited detailed post-acquisition integration plans. However, planning can only go so far. It is in the actual management of the post-acquisition phase that value is created or destroyed.

It would seem that the difficulties of the post-acquisition phase are beginning to be realised. It is now fashionable within some organisations to label acquisitions as mergers, partly in the hope that the term 'merger' will somehow convince employees of a partnership atmosphere and so remove potentially expensive post-acquisition difficulties. Whilst this seems rather optimistic, clearly businesses are becoming aware that the post-acquisition phase can present serious problems.

CHAPTER 1: SUMMARY

- We are currently in a major wave of merger and acquisition activity.
- The vast majority of evidence on acquisition performance shows that some 50 per cent fail.
- Pre-acquisition factors are only weakly associated with post-acquisition performance.
- The management of the post-acquisition phase is a major determinant of success.

Notes

1   These figures undoubtedly understate the case as the values of many cross-border deals are not publicly known. The numbers of deals however are a more reliable measure of activity.

2   This figure may include domestic deals.

3   On average each company acquired 25.5 companies over a ten year period.

4   Performance measured as accounting return on assets, and stock market return.

5   This is not to say that carrying out turnarounds on acquisitions cannot be a successful strategy as a number of acquirers, such as The News Corporation and Hanson Trust, have achieved considerable success in this regard. However, on balance, unless the parent company has specific turnaround skills, turnarounds should be treated with considerable caution.

Why may there be problems in the post-acquisition phase?

INTRODUCTION

In this chapter we explore why there may be problems in the post-acquisition phase. These problems can arise as a result of either the acquisition process itself or the post-acquisition reality.

THE ACQUISITION PROCESS

Acquiring a company is *a process* and indeed may be part of a larger acquisition strategy. However, there is a strong tendency for the process to break down into parts. This creates structural problems and a lack of continuity, which result in significant difficulties in managing the post-acquisition phase.

These structural problems can be grouped into two categories:

- focusing on the deal; and
- the gap in the acquisition process.

FOCUSING ON THE DEAL

Momentum

In striving to close deals, a momentum often builds up, in terms of time and the commitment of resources. This can make it very difficult to walk away from a deal. Of course advisors would say that momentum is essential for closing a deal, otherwise issues to negotiate just proliferate and are never resolved. Part of a merchant/investment bank's role as lead advisor is to keep the ball rolling, so that the deal is not derailed by overwhelming complexity.

The City and investors' reactions to the deal also influence the companies. The stock market can play an important role in influencing management teams concerning the 'acceptability' of the deal and its handling. In the case of Electronics PLC,[1] the board openly admitted that they felt pressurised by City investors to make acquisitions, in order to conform to the City's perception of them as an acquisitive company, or face being down rated.

Stock market influence is not to be underestimated as shown by the performance of SmithKline Beecham after the failed merger talks with Glaxo Wellcome. Share prices fell sharply during the acrimonious aftermath despite the former's strong performance.

Organisations incur very substantial costs in launching acquisitions, both in fees and, perhaps more importantly, in top management commitment. This not only uses very substantial amounts of time, but also has a cost in terms of distracting that management's attention from running their own companies. This becomes more serious the smaller the company. There is also the issue of managerial reputation in that making acquisitions is largely seen as showing positive leadership qualities whereas being unable to complete deals is generally viewed negatively. For instance, Lord Hanson was accused of 'losing his touch' when he failed to acquire ICI, and following the abortive SmithKline Beecham/Glaxo Wellcome merger, *the credibility of both drugs makers and of their top executives ... was deeply tarnished*' (*Wall Street Journal*, New York, 25 February 1998).

There are therefore internal and external pressures which feed momentum, but it is a necessary evil in helping close deals. However, as Warren Buffet said of the previous acquisition wave, *the thrill of the chase blinded pursuers to the consequences of the catch*'. Momentum has some unhealthy characteristics, which can present significant difficulties in the post-acquisition phase. These are:

- reductionism
- fragmentation
- ambiguity.

Source: Jemison and Sitkin (1986)

Reductionism

The complexity of deals and the pressure of time generally result in an often unconscious selection process about which aspects of the acquisition to concentrate upon. In trying to manage the complexity of a deal, advisors will generally concentrate upon those aspects which are codified, can be verified and, in a worst case scenario, might be defended in court. So, for instance, the vast majority of time is spent on pouring over financial statements and legal contracts rather than on the other important issues necessary for the successful running of the businesses post-acquisition. Part of this screening process also results in less tangible issues being ignored or indeed not perceived at all. Verifiability and communicability can therefore assume more importance than criticality. Important, but less tangible issues such as cultural differences, environmental concerns, core capabilities and 'the corporate mind' can be overlooked or pushed to one side. Whilst 'soft issues' may have been pushed aside for the harder issues pre-deal, as we shall see later in the book, post-acquisition, *there is nothing "soft" about soft issues*'.

Fragmentation

Linked with the notion of reductionism is fragmentation. Particularly for companies that do not have much in-house experience of acquisitions, specialist advisors will quickly dominate the process of making an acquisition. Advisors will do their utmost to cover all the angles from their standpoint, and the acquiring top managers can quickly find all their time absorbed by the intricacies of financing or legal complications. In the words of one chief executive, *'Once the lawyers got involved, the complexity went up.'*

Owing to the complexity of the analysis and number of tasks to be accomplished, it is difficult for the acquirer to maintain a generalist's grasp of the transaction (Jemison and Sitkin, 1986). The problem of integrating a variety of over-specialised and fragmented views is quite common. In the words of one CEO,

> *During the negotiations, there were so many people involved, it was hard to tell who was doing what, let alone how all their efforts would tie together.*
>
> (Jemison and Sitkin, 1986)

The use of many advisors can cause companies to miss the big picture and have a false sense of confidence. Of course, once the deal is completed, the post-acquisition period will quickly reveal the holes.

Ambiguity

In attempting to conclude the deal, areas of ambiguity may remain on closure. Ambiguity provides useful manoeuvring room in negotiations, opportunities to save face in public, and can help find common ground on seemingly intractable issues (Jemison and Sitkin, 1986). However, these ambiguities are more than likely to resurface in a virulent form in the post-acquisition phase, damaging pre-acquisition trust and potentially leading to escalating conflict. The ambiguity which might be essential during negotiation may be sowing the seeds for post-acquisition disruption.

THE GAP IN THE ACQUISITION PROCESS

Research by Angwin and Wensley of Warwick Business School and Ernst and Young (1995) shows that there is widespread acknowledgement across a spectrum of senior managers that there is a gap in the acquisition process between 'doing the deal' and managing the post-acquisition phase (*see* Figure 2.1). If this rift is not carefully managed, serious problems can occur.

Fig. 2.1 Simplified linear model of the acquisition process

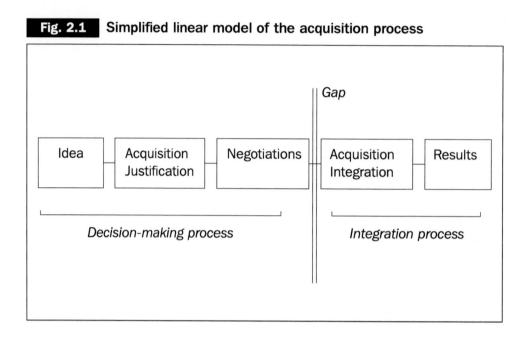

Disjunction between pre- and post-acquisition teams

Doing the deal requires a highly specialised set of skills for engaging with or hiring take-over advisors. In addition, negotiations are generally carried out at the highest level and, for reasons of secrecy, involve the minimum number of people. The problem with this approach is that once the deal is done, in many cases the deal doers move onto other things and a different set of executives are brought in at short notice and are often poorly briefed.

The costs of this disjunction are many. The executives managing the acquired company:

1 Can be badly informed about the overall purpose of the deal. With inadequate briefing, they will tend to just manage for broad financial targets.[2]

2 Are often not aware of verbal promises that might have been made to the acquirees: this can lead to significant breaches of trust, which can cause major management difficulties.

3 Are likely to encounter operational issues that were not fully considered, if realised at all, during the negotiations. This can seriously impair the purpose of the acquisition.

During the recent round of acquisitions in the water industry, one regional director was telephoned a day before the acquisition was due to close and asked whether he wanted to run the company. Once parachuted in, his brief was just a set of broad financial targets. A few weeks into the post-acquisition phase he began to uncover several serious operational difficulties which, in his words, '*any decent operations manager would have been onto like a shot if they'd had deeper involvement in the acquisition process*'.

One reason for the gap between executive types and their respective concerns is that, historically, integrating acquisitions has been seen as secondary to doing the deal. There is no doubt that deal doing is an heroic activity, the stuff of chief executives, whereas the act of integrating them is far less glamorous and longer term. In fact, an integrator is doing well just to achieve what was promised and expected in the deal. Behind this is a logic which suggests that the integration process is straightforward and can be handled by less senior employees. In addition, the skills necessary for doing the deal are different from those useful in managing the post-acquisition phase. For this reason, executives vital to the integration have tended to be excluded from negotiations.

So in the overall acquisition process there can be a gap between:

■ the level of executive involved; and

■ the skills being applied.

However, it is now widely realised that bad implementation can ruin strategies and indeed cause significant damage to both the acquired and acquiring companies. As pointed out in the introduction, the assumption that implementation will always be able to follow exactly from pre-acquisition plans is dangerous. In other words, one should *concentrate on the marriage, not the wedding*' (*The Economist*, 9–15 January 1999: 15).

You can never know everything about the target company

By definition an acquirer is unlikely to know everything about the target company. The level of 'awareness' will be determined by:

■ whether it is a private or public acquisition;

■ if public, whether it is friendly or hostile;

■ the extent to which the businesses are similar in nature;

■ the extent and quality of the relationship between the two companies before the acquisition;

■ the limits of due diligence and the nature of key knowledge.

Private or public acquisition

Public acquisitions have the advantage of giving the acquirers access to verified, good-quality information. There are excellent analysts' reports, industry analyses and often significant press comment, which can provide useful pointers. The limitation, however, is that information made available to a bidder by the target company is also to be made available to any other bidders or potential bidders, who may not be so desirable. For this reason, whilst the information available is of good quality, the preferred acquirer may have difficulty in obtaining information in important areas.

Acquirers of private companies gain much greater access to information, but it is likely to be of a poorer quality, as internal standards and depth of knowledge may be lower. In addition, gaining external information on smaller markets may be very difficult as sectors may not be well covered.

Friendly or hostile

As one might expect, gaining information from the target management team in a hostile acquisition is difficult, whereas an acquirer might reasonably expect an information room to be provided in a friendly acquisition of size. Nevertheless, even in friendly acquisitions, the acquired company's top management will, of course, be manoeuvring for the best advantage of their company, employees and investors. They will amply show the positive issues – and probably the negative ones which might be uncovered in any case – but are likely to skirt around other issues to maximise their negotiating advantage.

Similarities of businesses

There is common agreement amongst executives that to acquire companies in the same business area has apparent advantages in terms of understanding how the business works and knowing what questions to ask. Whilst this does have merit, it is important to sound a note of caution, as many executives have made substantial errors in assuming that acquired businesses work in *exactly* the same way as their own. As we shall see later, *'similarity is no guarantee of success'*.

On a more general matter of professionalism and corporate standards, acquiring managers may also assume that the target management and company have the same standards and views as themselves. Hence the acquiring management may be assured that certain issues are satisfactory, only to find later that this is true only in terms of the acquired company's standards and not in relation to their own.

Extent of the relationship before acquisition

Businesses which have had some form of in-depth relationship before acquisition tend to encounter fewer post-acquisition difficulties. In particular, an equity stake held for some time with a presence upon the board allows a more profound understanding of the target company and a more appropriate post-acquisition style.

The limits of due diligence and the nature of key knowledge

Pre-acquisition due diligence is used to gain an objective view of the acquired company and to overcome information asymmetries between acquirer and acquiree. However, acquirers can put too much faith in what pre-acquisition due diligence can actually achieve. In particular, due diligence may:

- not be sufficiently customised to the nature of the businesses involved. An acid test is to look at the due diligence list and ask whether the questions might also easily relate to a different type of business altogether;
- see the world in acquirer's terms and overlook important differences in the acquiree.

Issues which are not so easily handled are:

1 The need for lateral thinking – thinking outside of the box.

2 There can be an assumption that the quality of the acquiree's answers and professionalism will be of a similar level to the acquirer's. For example, in one engineering acquisition the acquired company assured the acquirer that certain components had been fully tested. Post-acquisition differences in the definition of 'fully' were rather expensive. This is not to say that the acquired company was deliberately misleading the acquirer, but that their standards in some areas did not match the exacting requirements of some of the acquirer's customers, which the acquirer had taken as the norm.

3 Appropriate data for un-codified and less tangible issues can be very difficult to extract. For instance, target employee attitudes and cultural nuances can be hard to fathom before acquisition.

Apart from the selective screening of information mentioned earlier, particularly in large, complex and international acquisitions, due diligence experts often have insufficient time and lack sufficient access to produce an ideal level of detailed analysis. For this reason, deal negotiators often push for as many warranties as possible. Whilst these legal mechanisms can offer a degree of protection, financial redress several years after the event is of little comfort when the post-acquisition integration process runs into difficulties.

The perceived value of due diligence across Europe was examined in a joint research project between Angwin and Ernst and Young (1997). A clear finding was that the most experienced acquirers had much lower expectations of what due diligence could achieve than less experienced ones.

Due diligence can only go so far and a prudent acquirer must expect to find some skeletons in the closet post-acquisition. In most cases, of course, these skeletons will cause a scare and be costly, but on occasion they can be positive. In one recent large media acquisition a number of items had been squirreled away by an over-cautious previous management. Upon acquisition, these items were discovered to be far more valuable than had hitherto been realised.

POST-ACQUISITION REALITY

One of the main advantages of making an acquisition is the speed with which the acquirer gains a presence within a market or ownership of complex resources. However, in buying companies, the acquirer is invariably taking on '*dross with the jewels*'. The extent and nature of this dross will become evident in the post-acquisition phase and can be quite different from what was expected. This can lead to value-destroying behaviour by acquirers and acquirees alike as their expectations fail to gel with reality.

Major issues relating to post-acquisition reality can be divided into the following categories:

- the acquisition is not as expected
- internal obstacles to post-acquisition management
- external pressures on post-acquisition management.

THE ACQUISITION IS NOT AS EXPECTED

Reasons why the acquisition is not as expected include:

- unpleasant surprises
- a lack of real understanding of the acquired business
- difficulties in achieving synergies.

Unpleasant surprises

Pre-acquisition screening of information may not give as good a view of the acquired company as those managing the post-acquisition phase might need. For this reason, there may well be unpleasant surprises, such as in the case of Ferranti's acquisition of International Signal Controls, where claims made about substantial contracts were not checked. These contracts turned out to be illusory, resulting in a massive hole in Ferranti's balance sheet and its ultimate demise. Another example is British and Commonwealth's £408m acquisition of the computer leasing company, Atlantic Computers. Post-acquisition the acquisition was found to be so riddled with liabilities that British and Commonwealth went into administration. Unpleasant surprises also abound in the purchasing of good businesses. In the acquisition of WordPerfect by Novell for $855m, a severe corporate culture clash between employees had such a deleterious effect upon the business that the latter was sold off for just $124m (*Wall Street Journal*, 12 January and 1 February 1996).

Severe corporate culture clash can be widespread, as was evident during the time of the 'Big Bang' in the City of London, where large banks began to pursue notions of becoming integrated financial houses by purchasing stockbrokers, merchant banks and other financial houses. In many instances, senior staff of acquired businesses left shortly after acquisition owing to fundamental differences over how the broking business should be run. For instance, the acquisition of Smith NewCourt PLC by Merrill Lynch caused significant culture clash and led to several high-profile departures such as Smith NewCourt's head of research and Merrill Lynch's head of strategy. Commenting on the recent wave of mega-mergers among banks, the Bank for International Settlements (BIS) showed that bank profitability had fallen in 12 countries despite the consolidation. The BIS blamed acquirers for 'systematically' underestimating organisational problems (*The Economist*, 28 August 1999 : 63).

If the acquired management intends to leave after the deal, the target company may have been drifting through lack of direction and energy at the top. There may also have been cut backs on necessary investment, as the length of time needed to see a return would be beyond the incumbent management's intended time with the company. Poorly maintained property, lack of training and inadequate systems will undoubtedly have an effect upon staff morale and will present the acquirer with an up-hill task to achieve motivation. There may also have been a skill loss, which may be difficult to restore.

A lack of understanding of the acquired company

Opportunistic purchases or bargains may mean inadequate consideration of how the acquired company operates and how it will really fit with the parent.

Linked to the above may be misconceptions held by the acquired company of the way in which they would work with the new parent after acquisition. If post-acquisition management styles are not considered pre-deal, then again, the acquired company may quickly deteriorate.

During the recent round of acquisitions by utility companies following privatisation, a successful engineering company making filters was acquired. During the negotiations it was clear to the top management of the target company that the utility company saw them as part of a vertical diversification strategy. Post-acquisition, it rapidly became clear that this was more or less a fiction, as the acquired company's sales continued to be to other players in the industry rather than the new parent and there was little dialogue between themselves and head office. With hindsight, the strategy of the utility was clearly one of setting up barriers against potential re-nationalisation by the next government rather than managing its many acquisitions.

A common difficulty occurs when an acquired business of apparently the same type reveals that similarities on the surface conceal fundamental differences.

A cable casing manufacturer in England with customers across the UK acquired a Scottish competitor whose customers overlapped its own. There was very little difference between the two products. Confident in the knowledge that they understood the target's business, the acquiring managers made the acquisition and then ran into very significant post-acquisition difficulties. The cultures within the two companies were quite different and each regarded the product and their selling of it in quite different ways: the Scottish company regarding it as a more sophisticated offering than the company based in England. As a result, the former's sales force had a higher standing in the company than the latter's and were rewarded more substantially with better pay and benefits.

Post-acquisition, premises and teams were amalgamated and managers of the acquirer were arriving at work in very modest cars, whereas their subordinates turned up in Range Rovers. It was deemed to be too expensive to upgrade all employees' cars and benefits to the acquired company's standards, and downgrading acquired employees' benefits would have led to rapid defections. A gradual attrition of one or incremental increase of the other would not solve the immediate tensions thrown up on day one under new ownership. The company car issue then was only the visible tip of an iceberg!

Not understanding the acquired company can lead to significant and expensive problems when the acquired company tries to work with the new parent.

Difficulties in achieving synergies

The language of many take-overs is couched in rational economic terms. In particular, we often hear of realising economies of scale and creating value through other synergies. However, despite the best efforts of both companies, these synergies may not materialise, or not at the rate at which they were expected.

Realising synergies is such an elusive issue that for many years the word synergy was almost banned. It is perhaps not surprising then that acquirers often find themselves unable to realise the synergies they expected.

In broad terms we may think of synergies as falling into two camps. There are gains from:

- cutting costs, as there will be duplication of resources between the two companies; and
- leveraging capabilities by transfers between the companies.

Cost cutting, or 'cost outing' as it is now becoming known, aims to rationalise two companies' resources whilst maintaining revenues. For instance, there is generally no need for two head offices; factories may be closed to increase utilisation in the remaining ones; the number of employees can be substantially reduced; suppliers can be rationalised.

The problem, however, is that merged firms may not be able to cut their costs as fast as their competition. Recent research by Santomero (1999) has shown that merged banks in America have generally cut their costs more slowly than their non deal-making peers. Also of concern in terms of mega-acquisitions is whether there is a size beyond which real economies of scale are outweighed by the organisational costs of achieving them.

When creating value through the transfer of capabilities, what can seem to be logical on paper can present very considerable difficulties in practice. For instance, where banks, building societies and insurance companies have merged, cross-selling of products was supposed to be a clear and straightforward synergy. However, many have found this surprisingly difficult to achieve, owing to quite subtle differences in how the organisations viewed such products. This is illustrated in Case study 2.1 by the views of the chief executive of a life assurance company five years after it was acquired by a leading building society.

Case study 2.1

Difficulties in realising synergies

'To achieve cross-selling, the Life company paid a commission to the Building Society to sell our products. The Building Society then paid their employees to sell, out of that money, and the balance to cover the cost of running the Building Society operations. We didn't control the Building Society person or the costs of selling, although we did train them, but we controlled the commission rate paid. However, it was certainly not as easy as anyone thought.'

'The whole culture of Building Societies is not to sell. If you wanted to do something, we'll give you some money, if you want to take the money out of your pocket we'll take it. You've got to ask us to do it. We're not going to be proactive and try and sell you things – goodness – ooh it's not the done thing at all! We're a mutual organisation we are – we're not there to make money!'

'This attitude is changing today, but nevertheless very few people have yet done it properly or well. The big question mark I have about the success of bank assurance is the ability to sell. At the end of the day, people aren't comfortable selling in the branch.'

Another area where compatibility is critical is information technologies and systems. In 70 per cent of merged companies, information systems are combined immediately after the deal, and up to 90 per cent eventually combine such operations into a single data centre and so reduce costs (Ball, 1988). The evidence, however, from Coopers and Lybrand (1993) is that in 40 per cent of acquisitions, integrating information systems is a significant difficulty. All too often the integration of information systems and technologies is not considered early enough, resulting in unrealistic integration time-scales and budgets. Divergent technologies, incompatible data structures, ageing or badly documented software plus the tendency for planners to hand responsibility to operational staff without adequate briefing, account for significant disruption (McKiernan and Merali, 1995). The heaviest cost during implementation is often associated with software conversion (Carlyle, 1986), while hardware and communications are relatively easy.

INTERNAL OBSTACLES TO POST-ACQUISITION MANAGEMENT

When an integration begins to encounter difficulties, the parent company may perceive in the acquired company:

- negative management attitude
- poor management practices
- employee resistance.

Management attitude in the acquired company

In Coopers and Lybrand's (1992) survey, the most commonly cited cause of acquisition failure was management attitude, with 85 per cent of interviewees mentioning this factor. For example:

> *The management culture was totally different. We take decisions quickly. They spend weeks in committees arguing over what should be done.*

Whilst the assumption behind this quotation is that fast decisions are better decisions, the important point is that these differences in management practice may conceal deeper differences about how the business should be run. This should cause acquirers to reflect *carefully* upon whether the businesses are indeed as similar as at first thought.

Poor management practices in the acquired company

This issue ranked fourth in Coopers and Lybrand's (1992) study. Poor management practices may not be obvious before acquisition as the target management team will have been spending their energies on negotiating the sale of their business rather than on demonstrating how they run it. In other words there may be more attention given to a snapshot view of the business, rather than to a process one.

After the acquisition, poor management practices may become apparent and present the acquirer with a difficult problem. This is particularly acute if the acquirer has purchased a business in an unfamiliar area or finds out that the business has significant differences from its own. The paradox is that the acquirer needs to intervene in the management of the acquired company but the acquired company's top executives will either resist this as they struggle to retain power, or depart, leaving the acquirer without any senior executives who really understand the customers and business. This situation occurs often in cross-border purchases of owner-managed firms in continental Europe, where the intention is to manage the firm at arm's length, so depending upon the quality of the incumbent management for post-acquisition performance. The owner manager, now enriched by the deal, may lose motivation, treat the business like a gentleman's club, allow less than rigorous standards, accept indifferent performance, and yet be very difficult to remove owing to protective legislation (Conversation with Andrew Collinson of Collinson Grant Consultants, 1998).

The management practices of owner-managed firms will quickly come to light should the top managers leave after acquisition. This is not to say that owner-managed firms are always badly run, but that they can be very quirky in nature and not fit easily into the larger company's pattern of operations. For this reason, acquirers need to be very sure of themselves if they are purchasing an owner-managed business where the owner manager is intending to leave upon the signing of the deal.

Employee resistance

Most of the problems adversely affecting the performance of merged firms are internally generated by acquirers and the dynamics of the new entity (Yunker, 1983). These self-inflicted difficulties are generally manifested in terms of employee behaviour in both the acquired and acquiring companies.

Employee uncertainty

Employees of both the acquired and acquiring companies need to be managed with considerable care. It is well known that, following acquisition, employees in the acquired company, in particular, are living in a time of considerable uncertainty. This uncertainty leads to fear of what may happen to their company, their job responsibilities and ultimately themselves. In one chief executive's view, *'they've been pushed down to the bottom layer of Maslow's hierarchy – their world is in turmoil, "How do I feed my family?"'*

This merger-related stress can be greatest for those who have given considerable commitment to the company over the years and yet cannot influence the post-acquisition process.[3]

Loss of employees and knowledge

Uncertainty, if not carefully handled, can lead the rumour mill to work overtime and result in very significant negative behaviours. In its weakest form this may just be apathy and a rise in absenteeism. However this can quickly escalate, with quality employees leaving the company. In the words of one chief executive, *'the best staff leave first as they're the ones with job offers piling up'*.

In sectors such as professional services, where most of the value of the business is embodied in highly-paid professionals, it is well known that once a merger or acquisition is announced the 'headhunters start circling'. With lucrative offers upon the table, key employees may well be tempted to leave if efforts have not been made rapidly to manage their expectations. Uncertainty and the fear, even if unjustified, of risk to their personal standing within the new group may tip the balance.

This loss can be serious for two reasons:

1 *Replacing key staff* – in certain industries it can be very difficult to replace key staff. Where the competitive advantage of firms lies mostly in personal technical knowledge, abilities and client relationships, such as in computer software businesses, the media, management consultancy, staff have a considerable significance for the prosperity of the business. As one managing director of a consultancy put it, *'if the key staff walk out of the door, what have you got?'*.

   Whilst there is a general tendency to concentrate upon individual employees and their importance, this can lead to the broader picture – how the individual fits into the organisation and helps make it work – being ignored. This is something of a double-edged sword, in so far as an individual may not only have some specialist skills but may also be a critical part of the way a team or indeed the company functions. Whilst it is difficult to find someone with specialist skills, it can be even more difficult to find someone who will fit into the organisation in an effective way.

2 *Loss of corporate memory* – if the acquirer loses several key employees, the loss is magnified beyond the sum of the parts. These employees take not only their specific skills but also their implicit understanding of how the organisation works and what its capabilities are. This can be viewed as a more general loss of corporate know-how or memory.

   In the current round of acquisitions in the computer industry, it is well known that keeping key staff is critical for the success of an acquisition. This link may well prove crucial in Lucent Technologies' agreed $20bn take-over of Ascend as they are said to have lost key staff in previous acquisitions which made integrating the business difficult. The loss of key individuals, then, can seriously undermine the *raison d'être* of the acquisition.

Passive resistance

If uncertainty persists and trust deteriorates between the acquired company's employees and acquiring company's employees, perhaps as a result of ambiguities in the negotiations, acquired employees will cling to the certainties of their past, when they knew where they stood. This can deteriorate rapidly into a 'them versus us' attitude, leading to a post-acquisition stand-off and passive resistance.

In the past it has not been uncommon to find, after a merger of professional service firms, the continuation of certain customs and attitudes which serve to preserve the identities of original cultures. For instance, in the City a large firm of solicitors which merged some years ago still maintains separate elevators for staff from the previous firms. At the extreme is the Japanese approach in the multiple mergers forming their largest banks. The original identities of each bank were enshrined in many duplicated head office functions such as personnel, as well as amongst executives within other departments, to reflect equal treatment and power balance. This led to very unwieldy institutions.

Organised resistance

Where trust breaks down and the workforce is organised in unions, in extreme cases there may be organised resistance in the form of strikes. This organised resistance can be effective in preventing changes that the acquirer feels need to be made. For instance, organised resistance was experienced by Carlton following its acquisition of Central Television, when it moved to close the Birmingham television studios. Such resistance can be costly, causing additional funding requirements, delays in the post-acquisition schedule, and poor publicity for the acquirer.

Where acquirers attract poor publicity or gain a negative reputation within industry for the way in which they handle the post-acquisition phase, they risk subsequent costs in later deals. A negative reputation for post-acquisition management will work against the acquirer where there is competitive bidding for a subsequent acquisition, in the tone and nature of those negotiations and the likelihood of difficulties in post-acquisition management.

In extreme cases of disaffection, employees actions may damage the core of the business by sabotaging equipment, ruining customer relationships, bringing in regulatory authorities to cast doubt on the company's reputation. Such damage will cause a decline in organisational productivity and operational effectiveness. Post-acquisition drift in the performance of the acquired company may result. There is also the very real risk of damage to the parent company with a drain on its managerial, financial and commercial resources as well as affecting its image amongst external stakeholders. Such negative outcomes can result in a change in strategic direction for the group as a whole.

REASONS FOR INTERNAL OBSTACLES TO POST-ACQUISITION MANAGEMENT

Employee resistance or managerial ineptitude is often blamed for the failure to achieve post-acquisition management objectives. These, however, are the symptoms rather than the causes. The internal causes of these difficulties can be seen as problems of strategic fit matching organisational fit. Where full integration is intended, this may expose issues of:

- relative standing
- corporate cultural differences
- national cultural differences
- inappropriate integration design
- poor implementation.

Relative standing

It is easy for the acquirer to cite the acquired senior managers' attitude as a major cause of acquisition failure, as they are in a powerful position to determine the nature of the game. However, the problem may be just as much with the acquiring top management, and may be signalling some profound underlying differences.

'Conquering heroes'

The deal will have shaped the acquiring and acquired management teams' expectations. However, after the deal many more parties become involved and those expectations may diverge rapidly. It is quite common for acquiring companies to feel like 'conquering heroes' and begin to impose their will upon their acquisitions. Middle managers will tend to feel that the acquired company is fair game and look for ways to increase their own influence. In turn, the acquired company can rapidly become demotivated when a supposed state of dialogue becomes a set of marching orders. A myriad of demands from the parent will result in the acquired company fire fighting rather than focussing upon the larger picture.

'The horse may learn to talk'

Acquired management may feel sufficiently threatened that they create obstacles to integration. In order to defend their business from what they perceive to be unthinking or strong headed interference, they will accept demands put upon them to avoid conflict and to be perceived as 'good guys'. However this may be a case of 'the horse may learn to talk'. A Greek King sentenced a subject to death. At this pronouncement the individual said that if the King spared his life, he would teach the King's favourite horse to talk. The King was intrigued and allowed the subject a one year stay of execution. The subject went away, pleased. A friend said to him 'you know you are not going to get that horse to talk', to which the subject replied, 'in a year, anything can happen. I may die, the King may die, the horse may learn to talk'.*

Acquired top management voice

For the top management of the acquired company, the relative standing of their business within the larger group is of great importance. This will generally be conditioned by absolute size and contribution to group profit. The top managers of significantly smaller or loss making companies are likely to make little impact at head office. If the acquired top managers do not have a voice at head office, particularly if their expectations from the negotiations had led them to believe that they would be an important part of the new group, then they and their employees will become demotivated, leading the business to underperform.

An example of this was a supposedly synergistic acquisition of a life assurance company by a major building society. Despite the promises of the negotiations, the chief executive of the life assurance company complained about the ingrained nature of the building society's way of doing business. In his view, *'we were nothing to them'*.

Another example, where the acquired company was making losses, is well reflected in the comments of the acquired chief executive of Transistor PLC who said,

I was exceedingly frustrated and mystified that, despite building this thing up over the last 13 years, I never had a discussion with any board member of Circuit Board PLC about the future of the company.

Business differences

What may appear to the acquirer as just different ways of managing the firm may reflect profound differences in the nature of the business itself. The acquirer may well have considerable confidence in producing a similar product but owing to differences in customer base, for instance, things may be done differently. This may manifest itself in management attitude which is then misinterpreted as awkwardness or inefficiency.

---

* I am indebted to Tony Helman, former Chief Executive of Datastream International for the insight offered by this Greek fable.

Corporate cultural differences

'The insidious hand of the past' pervades all businesses. The pattern of activities, behaviours and beliefs springs as much from engaging with the current business world as from the company's history. Often the acquired company's business is interpreted in the light of the acquiring company and current business conditions. This can lead to the acquirer overlooking important links between the way in which the acquired company operates and its deeply ingrained beliefs about how the business should be carried out. These beliefs rarely surface explicitly and are often manifested in apparently minor ways. However, when challenged, which normally occurs when the acquirer attempts to make changes in the post-acquisition phase, the true depth and complexity of these differences can emerge. This can then result in incompatibilities and expensive inefficiencies.

Case study 2.2 is an example of culture clash in two American banks that merged in August 1981.

Case study 2.2

Organisational culture clash

Despite a number of joint committees formed between the banks before the merger and several meetings between them, an analysis of all memos before the merger as well as interviews showed that 'no problems or potential problems were publicly anticipated'.

Almost immediately after merger, 'a "storming atmosphere" began to emerge. Organisational members of both banks began to experience a growing uneasiness concerning Merged bank and their position in the institution'. These feelings eroded rapidly the potential for co-operation. 'We–they' feeling intensified, with employees of each organisation seeing the other as 'the invading enemy'. First came negative stereotyping and then an 'arm wrestling phase' with senior employees jockeying for position. This had the unintended dysfunctional effect of contributing to friction at the merged operational level. Despite pre-acquisition promises of no job losses, layoffs followed, with the 'Christmas Massacre', which resulted in profound and widespread distrust of the new leadership and organisation.

> *The massacre really destroyed any motivation. People stopped caring about the bank.*
> *When you really don't care, you're not going to put any effort into what you are doing.*

Organisational costs from culture clash ranged from subtle slowdowns in customer service to whistle blowing, which led to an investigation by the FBI and Justice Department, a fine, and negative publicity in the local press. The merged bank did not return to profit until four years after the merger, in marked contrast to the industry in general.

Source: Buono and Bowditch (1989: 30–37)

Differences in national culture

In some ways national cultures are a sub-set of the above, although more readily recognisable. With cross-border acquisitions now accounting for an estimated 25 per cent of all global acquisition activity, the issue of managing cross-border is increasingly important.

Acquiring in a different country can cause difficulties if acquirers are not primed. Differences in language, rules and regulations are the more visible aspects of national cultures, but it is the less tangible, un-codified issues that can cause significant problems. These can lead to erroneous assumptions, frustrations and the erosion of trust. For instance, difficulties in the Metal Box–Carnaud merger have been attributed to differences in national cultures, with the autocratic management style of the French clashing with the more participative style of the British (*Financial Times*, 12 September 1991).

Variations in national cultures may be manifest in surprisingly slight ways but have considerable impact. Pharmacia of Sweden and Upjohn of America in 1995 were attempting to cut costs and match drugs portfolios. However, additional costs and significant amounts of time were wasted on rows over 'American' practices such as banning alcohol at lunch (*The Economist*, 9–12 January 1999: 23). The Americans angered the Swedes by scheduling meetings during the latter's national holiday period, and there was friction between decision styles as the Swedes penchant for open discussion and concensus did not mesh well with the American's directive, detailed–oriented style. Fears that one side would dominate if corporate head offices were consolidated in one country prompted the merged businesses to set up a new head office in London. However, as neither side closed their offices in Sweden and the US, this only created a new layer of management that duplicated existing structures (*Financial Times*, 20 February 1998). Such national differences are well illustrated in Case study 2.3 by the comments of the MD of an acquisition in the UK by a Swiss company.

Case study 2.3

National cultural differences

'The Swiss CEO came over and looked at the coffee lounge. He used to say, "What are they doing?". I'd reply, "they're having a cup of coffee". In fact the employees were trickling off the benches to grab a coffee. This was a total anathema to the Swiss. And it's true, when I went to their place in Switzerland – you can't even smell coffee, never mind a coffee break. They couldn't understand this British wanting to have coffee breaks. They thought it was almost, you know, lazy.'

'Another example was when I told them we'd be off on Monday, so there'd be no point in ringing. "What is this?" he asked. I said, "it's a Bank Holiday". "Bank Holiday?" he said. "Do you know, we have this in Switzerland too, but the employee must make the appointment with his manager and say he wishes to take the day off to make a protest. Nobody in your company does this..?!" I thought bloody hell, it's Herr Flick! And they really had a problem in understanding the British way of doing business. Actually I think we were pretty hard working and efficient. We just worked in a different way.'

There is some evidence that some national cultures work better together than others and there appears to be a link in the quality of information available before the acquisition. Following in the wake of the opening up of Eastern Europe, there has been a sustained level of acquisition by West European companies. However, there have also been significant frustrations, as shown by one German executive in the early days of cross-border activity, *'In Eastern Europe it's almost criminal trying to deal with them. They deal in an illegal fashion, try to take advantage of you, lie – it's absolutely hopeless'*. In contrast, countries such as the USA, UK, Netherlands and Scandinavia are perceived by foreign acquirers to have few difficulties post-acquisition.

A survey by Angwin and Ernst and Young (1997) of 142 companies with turnovers greater than $150m in Europe's six most acquisitive countries looked specifically at the issue of risks perceived to be associated with cross-border acquisitions. One finding was that there was generally a preference for acquiring in neighbouring countries, but this was also perceived to present the greatest difficulty. In the words of one Swedish executive, *'the Nordic area is our home ground and better known, except for the Norwegians!'*. This difficulty may reflect greater experience of acquiring in those countries and so increased awareness of risks. When the executives were asked whether external factors such as market conditions, politics, regulations, or internal factors such as culture, language, morale were the greatest source of risk after acquisition, the majority said internal issues were more risky and this perception increased with volume of acquisitions made.

Whilst considerable attention is focused upon the difficulties of handling different national cultures, we believe that it is more the differences between companies rather than between countries that are the greatest cause of post-acquisition problems.[4]

Inappropriate integration design

Part of the conquering hero syndrome is the imposition of the acquirer's structure, systems and procedures upon the target company. This may be justified in the case of accounting practices, although often more extreme than necessary, in order for there to be a common language within the group. In other areas this can lead to costly problems.

This issue is often manifest when an acquirer raises its sights in the scale of the acquisition. Although it may have had considerable practice in purchasing companies, and treating them as bolt-on assets, it is quite a different thing to try to integrate something larger and more complex. The surprise of this revelation was clear in this finance director's comments about their latest and largest acquisition.

Head office said, 'it's easy guys, you just get rid of the management and integrate it'. But this business was three or four times the size of anything we had acquired before. We had never taken the whole infrastructure from PLC board level and sophisticated computer systems and many and varied businesses and split them apart. So I think we thought it was going to be very easy and very similar and it turned out to be a lot more complicated.

An example of a structural difference appeared during the merger of two consultancies. One had a strong regional approach, the other was organised along skill group or product lines. In the words of the chief executive, *'There was a mis-judgement in terms of forcing them (the latter structure) into the structure and we lost ground as a consequence'*. The cost was the loss of consultants, who had identified with their particular skill group and not a regional centre, and some clients.

For large international companies, structural issues can take on ferocious complexity where it is not at all clear how a hybrid structure can work. One fascinating case is the acquisition of Rowntree by Nestlé. In this instance Nestlé had a strong country-oriented structure, with considerable power in the hands of country managers, whilst Rowntree was achieving excellent performance through being product-focused. To adjust either one risked destroying critical competencies. The solution they chose may have been more of a negotiating strategy than a truly intended synthesis, with the Nestlé structure dominating and the Rowntree experience being encapsulated in a central chocolate advisory group to sit alongside country managers. Nestlé admits itself that it is an awkward structure, but it appears to be very successful and indeed may prove to be a catalyst for change in the whole group.

Poor implementation

Linked with inappropriate integration design is the way in which the implementation is carried out. If the acquisition is valued for its unique abilities, then to march in like Genghis Khan will destroy a lot of that value. Likewise, if the company is in need of a turnaround, then to spend time debating and considering options could result in losing the business. Whilst these two extremes seem straightforward, it is surprising how often the purpose and action seem not to coalesce as 'the troops' are not fully briefed, properly controlled or appropriately sensitised.

A vital component of effective implementation is communication, not just to the acquired company's stakeholders but also to the acquiring company's employees.

However, according to a survey by AMR/ICME consultants, communications plans were insufficiently considered by 75 per cent of their respondents. They give an example of the hostile bid by Fuchs, the German oil group which succeeded in its hostile take-over of Century Oils but made no satisfactory employee communications for six months. *'Morale collapsed, employees left and performance had still not met expectations five years after the acquisition'* (Rankine, 1998: 116).

To a large extent, the severity of internal obstacles will be determined by:

■ the extent to which it is intended to integrate the acquisition; and

■ the fundamental differences between the two companies.

These core issues will be revisited in the following chapters. There are also external pressures upon management teams in the post-acquisition phase.

EXTERNAL PRESSURES ON POST-ACQUISITION MANAGEMENT

External pressures can force the hand of executives in their management of the post-acquisition phase. Apart from generic external pressures on a business, which top management must always monitor most carefully, including macro-economic fluctuations, political influences, advances in technology and changes in social factors, external pressures will also arise specifically from the acquisition. These pressures will include:

■ external stakeholders' expectations of change

■ competitors' reactions

■ legal requirements.

External stakeholders' expectations of change

For the larger deals, the City's analysts and investors as well as the media can influence post-acquisition events. Although interest in the past has mainly centred on doing the deal and evaluating the promises of rival management teams, there is a gradual but perceptible move towards reviewing whether the winning team carries out its promises. For instance, the substantial coverage of the hostile Granada/Trust House Forte acquisition was only to be expected, but the media continues to review Granada's handling of the old Forte empire.

There is a clear sentiment amongst senior managers that they need to signal to the City that they are achieving the claims they have made for the target company. For this reason there is often a focus upon quick hits and visible achievements, although this may not have such a strong operational rationale.

Evidence of the City's influence is the negative effect on SmithKline Beecham's ratings when analysts made a comparison with the merger of Bristol-Myers/Squibb in the US. They were perceived to be integrating more slowly than comparable companies in the US. SmithKline Beecham's management pointed out significant differences between the handling of their merger and that of Bristol-Myers/Squibb.

> *Where analysts were focusing upon the immediate gains to be made from the merger and the quick hits that would add to earnings that year, management was trying to build a structure and a workforce that would be right for many years.* (Bauman, Jackson, Lawrence, 1997: 127)

Despite this sound explanation for different integration speeds, the analysts' verdict was, '"*Restructuring going slower than expected.*" *SB's share price tumbled*' (Bauman, Jackson, Lawrence, 1997: 126).

Other external parties may emerge as surprise 'stakeholders'. Pressure groups who anticipate negative outcomes from the post-acquisition integration – perhaps in its effects upon the natural environment, potential impact upon the local economy and society, or dilution of regional and even national culture – can cause significant problems.

Competitors' reactions

Competitors often view an acquisition of a rival as a golden opportunity to gain market share and win new customers. They are aware of the significant amount of management time needed to carry out a full integration and that their rival may well have their 'eye off the commercial football'. The time is ripe for new marketing campaigns, aggressive pricing tactics and rumour mongering to lure clients away. One example during the 1980s was the take-over of Hill Samuel bank by TSB. One of the first actions of other merchant banks was to trawl through Hill Samuel's client list, at that stage one of the finest in the City, to see whether any clients could be turned.

Legal requirements

Where there is a need to work through the competition authorities, it is generally viewed as an irritating obstacle to the work of getting on with integrating the acquisition. Many months are often needed for clearance from the Office of Fair Trading. However the irony is that this 'slack time' can, and often does, work to the advantage of the companies. Rather than standing still, it seems to force the companies to do as much as possible in preparation for the post-acquisition period whilst clearance is awaited. This enforced waiting period allows some detailed planning and preparation between the parties at many levels and appears to have a significant positive effect upon the quality of post-acquisition management as well as buying time with the City.

In conjunction with the external pressures that arise specifically from the acquisition itself, top managers naturally have to continue monitoring the external business environment.

The pre-acquisition strategy will have set out the strategic case for making the acquisition in terms of how the acquired company could add to the parent's stock of capabilities and resources. However, post-acquisition there will be a set of constraints on what can be achieved. The difficulties encountered will be a function of the extent to which integration is intended and the compatibilities between the two firms.

CHAPTER 2: SUMMARY

- Too many focus upon the wedding and not the marriage.

- The gap in the process impairs post-acquisition management.

- The acquired company may be different from what was expected.

- Many failed acquisitions encounter problems with differences in management attitudes, practice standards and employee resistance.

- Problems may reflect profound differences in relative standing, organisational and national culture, organisational structure, process difficulties and poor implementation.

- There will be external pressures from the markets, competitors, investors, pressure groups and in some cases the authorities, which can hinder integration efforts.

Notes

1 All companies have been anonymised to protect identities.

2 This is fine for conglomerate style businesses, but damaging if other synergies are intended.

3 Senior management, with the most to lose, may at least have a say in the future and probably have job opportunities elsewhere.

4 It is worth noting, however, that the range of integration styles for cross-border deals can be less than for domestic deals, which may protect the acquisition from the worst problems of integration.

3

Selecting an appropriate post-acquisition style

INTRODUCTION

This is a conceptual chapter, which suggests how the difficulties experienced by many acquisitions might well be avoided. We briefly review the main issues of strategic fit and organisational fit and then focus upon the tension between the two. Skilful management of this tension is at the heart of successful mergers and acquisitions.

STRATEGIC FIT AND IMPLEMENTATION

A great deal has been written on rational strategic motives for making acquisitions and we will not cover these here as they are a sufficiently complex subject to fill an entire book. It is important however not to buy into the assumption that specifying a strategic rationale will inevitably lead to perfect implementation and enhanced results.

Numerous consultancy reports seek to show how strategic rationales, such as market entry, vertical integration, market penetration, are linked with areas of post-acquisition change and so with post-acquisition performance. A number of issues are immediately apparent:

1 Conventional strategic rationales, such as 'market penetration', may have specific meaning for the board and investors, but merely indicate a whole range of integration possibilities for executives taking charge of the acquisition, rather than indicating a specific series of actions.

2 Conventional rationales understate the real complexity of motives and intentions.

3 The link between strategic fit and performance has yet to be established as it ignores the difficulties and moderating effect of post-acquisition implementation.

Strategic recommendations

These models often view strategic fit in market/product terms. This tends to produce clear implementation recommendations for just two situations: where markets and products are the same for each company, full integration is possible, and where they are different the approach will be 'hands-off'. This is probably why many executives tend to polarise acquisitions into 'substantial integration' or 'hands-off' approaches.

Where there are product/market overlaps between the two businesses, but these are not precise, then a whole range of integration options is possible. In such situations, conventional product/market frameworks are not sufficiently fine-grained to indicate appropriate integration styles.

A confusion of motives

Financial motives masquerading as strategic ones

Such motives may be employed to increase profitability or improve shareholder value. If acquirers will not address their own strategy squarely, and surface what lies behind these financial *outcomes*, or indeed choose to believe that financial outcomes are a strategy, then it is no small wonder that implementation, with few cues, can flounder.

Multiple motives

The vast majority of surveys and reports on acquisitions seek to identify single, rational motives for acquisitions. The reality is likely to be more complex. There may well be a variety of motives, some with rational strategic foundations as well as some relating to more personal concerns and aspirations of senior management. There may be further complications with the acquisition resulting from a political process within the acquirer so that there is no one clear sponsor with a clear set of objectives. Although senior executives would always wish to be portrayed as the instigator of major strategic decisions, the author is well aware of instances where companies have bowed to the external pressures of investors wanting to see immediate action. This complexity of motives often results in a confusion, or indeed absence, of signals to executives responsible for integrating the acquisition. They then face significant difficulties in prescribing appropriate integration approaches.

Not the 'real' motives

Where the strategic motives 'in currency' in the company and amongst shareholders are not the 'real' motives, then top management needs to be careful their employees don't end up believing the hype.

FACTORS AFFECTING STRATEGIC FIT

Even where the strategic logic is singular and genuine, there are many factors that can prevent it from translating into a successful outcome. These can be grouped into:

- constraints from the negotiations
- constraints of organisational fit
- environmental change.

Transaction negotiations

Overpaying

The classic problem often cited in take-overs is that the acquirer paid too much for the business. Although this may well be wisdom in hindsight to cover disappointment with post-acquisition results, there is no doubt that paying an inflated price puts significant pressures upon integration managers to find rapid means of generating returns. As all managers know, it is generally a lot easier to cut costs through disposals and redundancies than it is to generate new income. An inflated price then has a negative effect upon post-acquisition management by greatly restricting managers' scope and eroding acquisition employees' confidence. Swingeing cuts may produce an immediate uplift in returns but can seriously weaken the acquisition and destroy its long-term value.

Constraints of expectations and trust

Some broad *expectations* about how the acquired company will be managed post-acquisition may be set during negotiations and *trust* established at senior levels. All deals have areas of ambiguity which can only be resolved within the time frame by degrees of trust between negotiators. Where top management remains in the acquired company, the post-acquisition intentions of acquirers can be constrained by verbal agreements from the negotiations. This can work in two ways. The acquirer's senior negotiators may have made verbal agreements with target top management, which then restrict the scope for action available to the acquirer's implementors. Alternatively, the acquirer's implementors find themselves acting against the spirit of the negotiations, either unwittingly, owing to poor communications between themselves and the negotiators, or intentionally. This may serve to break the bonds of trust and so lead to significant resistance from the acquired company.

Organisational fit

Organisational fit is the main cause of disruption between strategic fit and acquisition performance. Chapter 4 discusses techniques and methods for diagnosing the potential for organisational fit. The main areas relate to differences in:

1 *National and regional culture* – where the companies are geographically distinct there can be surprising and quite difficult differences to manage.

2 *Organisational culture and managerial practice* – we take this to include differences in:

- organisational structure
- power structures
- control systems
- rituals and routines
- organisational symbols
- organisational stories.

As Chapter 2 illustrated, these differences, if not properly managed, can all result in significant upheaval in the workforce and disruption to business. Although it is difficult to quantify, estimates suggest that damage caused by culture disturbances, for instance, can cost 25–30 per cent in lost performance (Walter, 1985).

TENSION BETWEEN STRATEGIC AND ORGANISATIONAL FIT

The tension between strategic fit and organisational fit is at the core of acquisition performance. It can be exacerbated or moderated by the acquirer's experience in designing and managing acquisitions. Acquiring in a familiar post-acquisition style generally leads to realistic expectations of what is achievable. However, shifting from one style to another, often unwittingly, results in unrealistic expectations and many disappointments. The latter situation frequently occurs when companies introduce a step change in the scale and complexity of their acquisitions. For instance, the author has encountered many firms who believe themselves to be experts at integrating acquisitions, only to find on closer enquiry that their acquisitions have tended to be asset purchases rather than corporates. Consequently, they haven't encountered the complexities of integrating more complex structures and management teams, or sometimes the acquired businesses have been kept distinct unconsciously, through accident of geography, so that there has been little integration to speak of. When these firms, with false confidence, have then embarked on the full integration of a sizeable acquisition, they have encountered very significant difficulties.

Additional contributors to tensions are the expectations of the acquired company and its employees. These may be influenced by previous experiences of acquisition and will certainly be shaped by the way in which the acquirer takes charge of the acquisition. Managing employees' expectations is discussed in the following chapter.

Acquisition integration does not take place in a vacuum, although it is surprising how many integrators act as though it does! There are important shifting external pressures.[1] To mention just a few, shareholder expectations will be shaped by their comparisons with 'similar' integrations and broader concerns, the media will search for topical angles, competitors will undoubtedly declare 'open-season' in their hunt for new customers, communities may protest at potential local impact, and encompassing them all, the macro-economy can transform business trading conditions both for good and ill.

The tension between strategic fit and organisational fit can therefore be influenced by:

■ the acquirer's actual or perceived experience of managing corporate acquisitions;

■ the management of corporate and employee expectations;

■ shifting environmental pressures.

Figure 3.1 summarises the many influences discussed so far which impact upon acquisition outcome.

Fig. 3.1 Influences upon post-acquisition performance

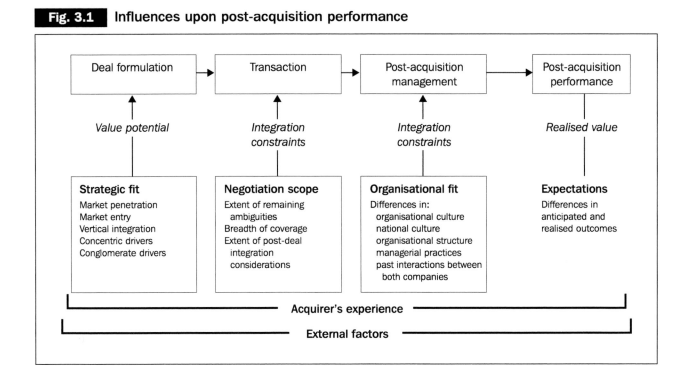

KEY DIMENSIONS IN ACQUISITION INTEGRATION

Whilst Figure 3.1 provides a useful conceptualisation of the influences upon acquisition outcome, we need to improve the links between strategic fit and organisational fit. To achieve this, we need to convert the conventional notions of the former into more helpful post-acquisition terms. There are two key issues to consider:

- how to create value from the newly acquired company;
- how to avoid damaging the value in the newly acquired company whilst attempting to create value.

How to create value from the new acquisition

Bringing two firms together will create potential benefits from greater size. These include:

- increased power in purchasing
- increased market presence
- lower financing costs
- greater financial opportunities
- increased stature and reputation
- greater stability in the business.

These benefits from increased size do not require a managerial process in transferring capabilities between organisations (Haspeslagh and Jemison, 1991: 29).

From a managerial perspective, creating value can be achieved by:

- sharing resources
- transferring functional skills
- transferring general management capability.

(Haspeslagh and Jemison, 1991: 28)

Through these exchanges, the sum of the parts may exceed the value of the companies on a stand-alone basis. Value is created by interaction between the capabilities and resources of both companies.

1 *Sharing resources* – value can be created by rationalising operating assets so that economies of scale, such as increasing the utilisation of one factory whilst closing another, or economies of scope, such as sharing distribution channels, can be achieved. Part of the benefit from both is likely to be in de-duplicating assets. Intangibles such as brands and corporate reputation can also be shared to advantage.

2 *Transferring functional skills* – transferring skills between companies can improve competitive positions. These can result from improving practices within functions, processes across functions, and applying support functions more broadly, such as using R&D to develop products in the new acquisition.

3 *Transferring general management capability* – such capability transfer would range from leadership and strategic goal setting to strategic, financial and human resource planning. As with transferring functional skills, this can be a two-way street, with the acquired company also supplying the acquirer with general management ability.

Knowledge transfer

*'Knowledge has become **the** resource, not a resource'* (Drucker, 1993: 6). Its value is that it is difficult to create and imitate. *'The process by which it is created and utilised may be the key inimitable resource'* (Schendel, 1996: 3). Mergers and acquisitions can create value by harnessing and transferring knowledge between companies and there is empirical evidence to suggest that there is a positive relationship between knowledge transfer and success (Angwin, 1998b).

The rise in the importance of knowledge transfer may reflect the recent occurrence of mega-mergers between professional service firms where much of the value of the business is based on knowledge in people's and teams' minds rather than in tangible assets. The particular importance of tacit as opposed to codified knowledge is that it is far more difficult for a competitor to imitate and therefore can lead to sustained competitive advantage. However, there can be significant difficulties in transferring knowledge between organisations.

Obstacles to capability interaction

There are often costs in transferring and sharing capabilities and resources. When operating resources are combined, there may be a loss of effectiveness if the overlap in activities is poor. For instance, where insurance companies and banks have merged, merely adding insurance products to those already sold through bank branches initially resulted in poor sales of the former and a less effective branch staff.

It is critical to realise the extent to which the functional skill to be transferred is dependent upon its *context*. Many mistakes are made in this area as acquirers and consultants often take a very narrow view of a particular skill or technique. This lack of appreciation of 'embeddedness' often means that the skill, when transferred, fails.

In terms of transferring knowledge, a useful study by Szulanski (1997), on the transfer of best practices intra-firm, gives some useful insights on the obstacles that may be encountered (see Table 3.1).

Table 3.1 Sources of difficulty in transferring best practices intra-firm

Most important

> The recipient was unprepared to recognise the value of a practice, assimilate it, and apply it to commercial practice

> The recipient lacked understanding of the practice

> Poor relationship between parties

> The recipient lacked motivation

Least important

Source: Derived from Szulanski (1997)

Note: A further factor which could temporarily outweigh the others was the 'perceived reliability of the recipient'.

In mergers and acquisitions, knowledge transfer presents particular difficulties when the bases differ fundamentally in form and content. This is most evident where the difference is between a firm based upon codified knowledge and a firm based upon tacit knowledge. In professional service firms, where knowledge is power and generally held widely amongst a substantial body of partners, this difference has wide-ranging implications for the success of integration. Tacit knowledge cannot be objectively valued and so results in both firms forming subjective judgements upon each other's knowledge. In the struggle for power, this can lead partners to undervalue what they do not comprehend and to perceive the other's knowledge base as 'illegitimate'. This can represent an impediment to knowledge transfer. For instance, partners of a firm based upon codified knowledge are likely to view those in a firm based upon tacit knowledge as 'intellectual butterflies', achieving success by the use of 'smoke and mirrors' rather than by anything more substantial, whilst the latter are likely to view the former as 'grease monkeys' or 'plumbers', emphasising a more pedestrian and lower status of knowledge (Empson, 1999). Such devaluation only serves to create barriers to consensus and the transfer of knowledge.

The 'embeddedness' of behaviour and the difficulty of transferring knowledge and behaviour are shown in Figure 3.2. Single experience (Content) and universal framework (Alignment) approaches to transfer are shown to often result in 'bounce back' as they hold context-free assumptions and so hit contextual barriers such as organisational politics and entrenched cultures.

To achieve greater success, Hsiao (1998) recommends that the transfer process must move to a third level (Dynamics) where there is greater collective reflection on the frame. In addition to moving through these levels there are also barriers in terms of individual perceptions and understandings. Individuals need to move beyond their understanding of patterns of actions to obtain a broader view of how those actions are part of a wider social system. They need to perceive the arena where employees' individual perceptions interact collectively. In other words, the success of transfer depends upon the understanding of 'conflicting frames' of reference. The key issue then is to shift the mindset of managers from searching for 'rational resolutions' to 'reflective interaction'. This deeper understanding will greatly improve communication between key parties and allow this greater reflection to take place.

Fig. 3.2 The three paths of transfer behaviour

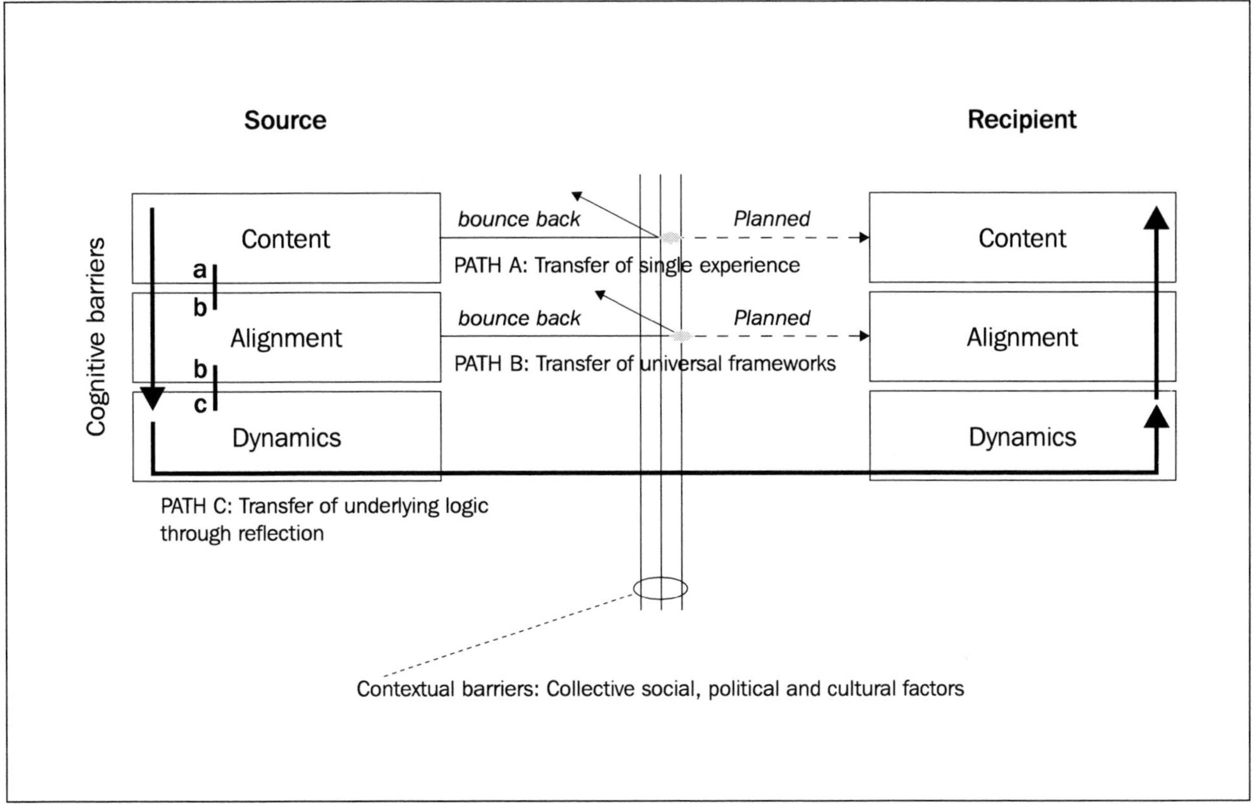

Source: Hsiao (1998). Reprinted by kind permission of the author

How to avoid damaging the value in the acquired company

Whilst exchanges between companies may offer the potential for creating value, there is also a cost. As with the Victorian gift ethic, which made the receiver of the gift beholden to the giver, such transfers from the acquirer to the acquired company can assume negative characteristics. Where the two companies are in similar business areas, transfers to the acquired company may begin to make it appear inferior and its morale may be undermined. The acquirer might also begin to assume an unjustifiable superiority in all things. Where the businesses are in unrelated areas, transfers may take on a much more corrosive quality.

An acquired company's valuable capabilities may easily be destroyed by the acquirer if the latter's assumed superiority results in interference beyond their real ability. It is vital therefore for the acquired company to be protected from such interference where it possesses unique and valuable capabilities. This protection is achieved by 'ring fencing' the acquisition: setting appropriate levels of strategic and financial independence. It is vital to ensure that the management of the acquired company is sufficiently powerful to control interaction between the two businesses. In many cases it is advisable to set up a 'gate keeping team' (Haspeslagh and Jemison, 1991) specifically for the purpose of moderating demands and exchanges between the companies.

Obstacles to strategic independence

There are two main difficulties in achieving the strategic independence of the acquisition. The first is handling the 'conquering hero syndrome' where there is a need for high levels of capability interaction between the companies to create value. Executives in the new parent will undoubtedly wish to assert themselves over the acquired company in terms of power and procedures and yet, if not controlled, this can lead to value destruction in the acquisition.

The second difficulty is the actual setting of the level of strategic independence. As an in-depth case study analysis by Wensley and Angwin (1996) of large acquisitive companies in the UK showed, top executives had difficulty in setting appropriate levels of autonomy for their acquisitions. Where the intention is to maintain the capabilities of the acquired company, too little autonomy results in the erosion of value. Where the intention is to integrate fully, too much autonomy results in power struggles and implementation difficulties.

Post-acquisition integration styles

These two critical issues of creating value and avoiding damaging the acquired company can be represented as:

1 Setting an appropriate level of *capability interaction*: the extent to which the acquiring company wishes to share and/or transfer capabilities to create value from the acquisition.

2 Determining the level of the acquired company's *strategic independence*: assessing whether to maintain the acquisition's particular configuration of capabilities and resources and so allow them to keep their strategic discretion or to subvert the acquisition's configuration to the acquirer's purposes.

From these two dimensions we can generate a post-acquisition typology of four distinct integration styles (see Figure 3.3).

Fig. 3.3 Post-acquisition integration styles

		Acquisition's strategic independence	
		Low	High
Capability interaction	Low	Isolate	Maintain
	High	Subjugate	Collaborate

* This framework is derived from Haspeslagh and Jemison (1991)

The level of capability interaction then sets the tone for potential value creation, whereas the strategic independence of the acquired company controls the potential friction between the two organisations. This control is reflected in the speed with which integration can take place and, as the next section shows, each style has an implicit integration pace based upon the level of strategic independence allowed the acquired company.

WHICH STYLE OF POST-ACQUISITION INTEGRATION IS APPROPRIATE?

The post-acquisition style to be chosen will broadly reflect the tension between strategic fit and organisational fit. For small to medium-sized companies, a single style will suffice, although for large acquisitions, it is possible for different styles to be adopted where there are distinct business areas. So for instance, some parts may well be fully subjugated whilst others remain relatively untouched.

Characterising the four dominant styles of acquisition

The four dominant styles of post-acquisition integration are characterised below. These styles are developed further in Chapter 5, where there are detailed cases for illustration.

Isolate

An acquisition held in isolation is often in poor financial shape at the time of acquisition. It is kept at arm's length to avoid infecting the group. In most cases a turnaround strategy will be employed to restore it to a healthy condition, after which the business may well be sold. Owing to the poor state of the acquired company, post-acquisition actions tend to occur very rapidly, with the post-acquisition phase being relatively short. As an acquisition technique, isolation acquisitions are quite risky but, as with all turnarounds, success can be very marked.

Maintain

Acquisitions that are maintained are most often in unfamiliar business areas – perhaps classic unrelated take-overs. Acquirers avoid interfering in the running of these acquisitions and instead try to learn from the acquired company's achievements. There may be a modest amount of financial risk sharing but essentially the way in which value is created in the acquired business is by the parent company encouraging greater professionalism and positively influencing the ambition of the management group. The post-acquisition phase tends to be rather gentle and it can take years for real benefits to show.

Subjugate

Acquisitions that are subjugated rapidly lose their identity and form and are subsumed within the parent group. Such acquisitions are often based upon clear similarities between both companies, so that amalgamation will bring economies of scale and scope. The integration process is complex, potentially occurring throughout all aspects of the business. The post-acquisition phase of subjugation acquisitions tends to occur quickly and bring rapid results.

Collaborate

Acquisitions that are collaborative see the acquired company having considerable independence from the new parent. The acquired company has its own head, but future projects and arrangements show joint efforts for the benefit of the group. Over time there is substantial interchange of capabilities, but this is a gradual process. Collaborative acquisitions are difficult to manage, there are substantial risks and the benefits are long term.

In theory, collaborative acquisitions offer the greatest potential for gain (Haspeslagh and Jemison, 1991). However the gains require the acquired company to retain a high degree of strategic independence, in order to retain the configuration of its core capabilities, whilst at the same time experiencing interaction of resources with the parent. This is something of a paradox, as the acquired company, in order to receive resources from the acquirer, loses some of its precious independence and has its capabilities threatened.

Consistency and routines

Selecting a post-acquisition style will need to take into account the quality of the acquirer's analysis allowing consistency of approach, as well as experience with integration.

There is evidence to suggest that consistency of approach to acquisition management is important for successful outcomes. Where there is consistency between the researchers' objective view of the integration, the company's perceived mode and the actual integration that took place, the acquisitions are high-performing (Haspeslagh and Farquhar, 1994). Problems occur where companies mis-assess the integration at the pre-acquisition stage and then have to adapt their integration mode over time. The worst acquisition encountered suffered from a mis-management gap where, although the assessment was appropriate, the company was organisationally incapable of the implementation (Haspeslagh and Farquhar, 1994: 434–6).

Empirical evidence suggests that experience with integrating acquisitions has an effect upon the style and degree of integration pursued by the acquirer. Higher levels of integration take place where acquirers have a codified, post-acquisition 'routine' of how this may be accomplished. The importance of this observation is that the knowledge for integrating acquisitions is related more to the replication of past decisions (routinisation), rather than to variations in the resource characteristics of the acquired company (Singh and Zollo, 1997). In this sense experience may be less helpful than anticipated, and could have negative effects.

ACQUISITION STYLES, OCCURRENCE AND SUCCESS

Post-acquisition style occurrence

Collaborative acquisitions would appear to have the greatest potential for creating value, as the core capabilities of both companies are maintained and there are value-creating opportunities in their interaction. We might therefore expect this acquisition style to dominate acquisition activity. However, as a large survey by the author of acquisitions in the UK, 1991–4 has shown, this is not the case (see Figure 3.4).

Fig. 3.4   Distribution of post-acquisition integration styles in the UK, 1991–4

		Acquisition's strategic independence	
		Low	High
Capability interaction	Low	**Isolate** 26%	**Maintain** 49%
	High	**Subjugate** 16%	**Collaborate** 9%

Source: Angwin (1998b)

Executives when speaking of acquisition styles tend to lean either towards the maintenance model of stand-alone management, or the subjugation model of full integration. As Figure 3.4 shows, whilst there are good grounds for discussing the maintenance style, which accounts for nearly half of all acquisitions, and subjugation acquisitions, which represent 16 per cent of acquisitions, our other styles are also well represented in the UK.

Isolation acquisitions accounted for 26 per cent of acquisitions. This is surprising, as this type of acquisition has traditionally been overlooked in the acquisition literature. The attraction of this acquisition style may be that, as it is managed at arm's length, it is managerially easier to handle. As isolation acquisitions are often financially weak, they can often be bought cheaply and, as the years 1991–4 encompassed a recession, this may have been an attractive, and in some cases the only, route to rapid expansion.

Theory suggested that collaborative acquisition would be a popular style, as it offers the greatest potential for value creation. However, the figure of around 9 per cent of all acquisitions was smaller than expected. This is surprising and suggests that, although this style holds out promise of substantial rewards, there are substantial difficulties in managing the paradox of transferring capabilities whilst maintaining levels of strategic independence.

Post-acquisition style success

With collaborative acquisitions in theory offering the potential for greatest rewards, and acquisitions with low capability interaction offering lower rewards, we might expect firms to concentrate upon the former and for these to be judged most successful. However, as we have mentioned, risks also seem to run in parallel with the rewards and this reduces the attractiveness of high interaction styles: transferring capabilities may well cause value destruction.

In examining which acquisition styles are more successful, we need to recognise that the views of top executives change over the life of an acquisition. In particular it is not unusual for top executives to be keen to talk about the success of the acquisition integration shortly after the deal, or much, much later. It is often critical to meet shareholder and city expectations and we would argue that there is often a significant disjunction between the messages transmitted from the tops of companies and the reality within the organisation during the post-acquisition phase. For this reason, where there have been attempts at substantial integration there is a noticeable reticence amongst top executives to talk about integration around the 18 months to 2 year mark, when the first unintended effects of change have begun to be felt and very considerable demands are put on management time.

As different styles offer risks and rewards and require varying amounts of time and effort to execute, we may expect to find some styles more successful than others. However, based upon broad perceptual measures, there is no empirical evidence to show that this is the case. For the moment then, we should think of these acquisition styles as being 'horses for courses'.

CHAPTER 3: SUMMARY

- Which integration styles are possible will be determined by the tension between strategic logic and the constraints of organisational differences.

- There are four main post-acquisition integration styles:

  isolate

  maintain

  subjugate

  collaborate.

- The appropriate integration style will be determined by the key decisions on:

  1 how value is to be created from the acquisition;

  2 the importance of maintaining the capability configuration of the acquired company.

- Value is created by the interaction of capabilities between the two companies.

- Acquired company capabilities are protected through high strategic independence from the acquirer.

- The style chosen and consistency of approach will be influenced by the quality of analysis and the level of 'routinisation' within the acquirer towards integration.

- There is no one best post-acquisition style, as they achieve different ends

Note

1 In certain industries this list of external pressures can be very extensive indeed, including such areas as changes in the physical environment, political interventions and pressures, legal restrictions and changes, technological developments, pressure group interventions, social change.

Taking charge of the new acquisition

INTRODUCTION

The immediate danger upon taking charge is a post-acquisition vacuum. There is a tremendous expectation of change amongst stakeholders and a vacuum will cause uncertainty and fear to grow. It is imperative, therefore, to show clear and confident handling of the acquisition immediately after completion by:

- hitting the ground running
- stabilising the acquired company.

Explicit planning, before acquisition, for the post-acquisition phase is vital for a smooth transition. Preparation should start well before the deal is signed and there may also be a window of opportunity between signing and completion for more detailed considerations. The depth and extent of the preparation, however, will be influenced by the amount of access to the target available to the acquirer before completion and the degree of integration intended.

In this chapter we shall look in turn at issues specific to the post-acquisition phase in:

- pre-signing preparation
- pre-closing window of opportunity
- immediate 'taking charge' actions.

PRE-SIGNING PREPARATION

Chapter 2 showed that acquisitions problems such as the gap in the process can lead to poor consistency between pre- and post-deal actions. To achieve continuity, acquirers should ensure that:

- a senior executive is appointed specifically to oversee and be responsible for the whole acquisition process;
- pre-acquisition planning specifically considers taking charge of the acquisition and further integration.

Appoint a senior executive to oversee the acquisition

From the acquirer's point of view, it is essential that there is continuity through the acquisition process so that the objectives of the acquisition flow through into the post-acquisition phase. The appointment of a senior executive to oversee and be responsible for the entire process helps avoid the problem of deal doers exiting once the deal is closed and a new team arriving and defining their own task. A senior, committed executive can counter the problem of fragmented perspectives, ensure continuity of integration and keep the spirit and purpose of the acquisition alive.

The executive has to be senior in order to be involved in all the acquisition negotiations and for notice to be taken of his views in the post-acquisition phase. All too often we hear of a head office manger being given this enormous responsibility and then being given the run-around by senior line executives. Ideally the senior executive will have a strong commercial understanding of both businesses, rather than just a financial appreciation. This should sharpen the perception of potential operating difficulties post-acquisition.

This critical role can be very demanding indeed and have far-reaching consequences for both companies. Its importance is underlined at GE capital where integration management is perceived as a full time job and the task of integration is recognised as a distinct business function (Arkansas, et al., 1998). The senior integration executive then should not be expected to take on this role in addition to all his other responsibilities.

Ensure high quality planning before the acquisition for the post-acquisition phase

Chapter 2 identified a strong positive link between pre-acquisition planning for the post-acquisition phase and post-acquisition performance (Shanley, 1994). Coopers and Lybrand (1992) showed that detailed plans for post-acquisition integration were one of the most frequently cited reasons for acquisition success. Chapter 3 showed that where acquirers were clear and consistent in their pre-acquisition assessment of the post-acquisition phase and their post-acquisition actions, and had an objective view of integration style, the post-acquisition phase was more successful than where acquirers were inconsistent (Haspeslagh and Farquhar, 1994). The value of planning for the post-acquisition phase, even where the detail available is limited, is that it is a useful discipline for thinking ahead and in itself begins to create the conditions for change.

Whilst the detail possible in pre-acquisition planning will be determined by the acquirer's level of understanding of the target business, the extent of access to the target company before ownership and the strategic intentions behind the deal, the acquirer can work out an appropriate acquisition style based upon the framework shown in the previous chapter. This will give rise to an appropriate set of actions, which can be divided into:

- 'immediate taking charge' actions (see p.65); and
- 'subsequent post-acquisition actions by integration type' (see Chapter 5).

Whilst it is not appropriate to discuss planning techniques in any detail in this book, a number of broad issues may usefully be considered, although they would need to be tailored to the specific nature of the industry.

It is important to note that, whilst the strategic intent behind the acquisition may be framed in product and market terms, in many cases the implications for amalgamating organisational structures, functions and processes are not entirely straightforward. As a consequence, in thinking about the post-acquisition phase, it can be valuable to reconsider what the acquisition means from other perspectives, such as the compatibility of capabilities and resources. In attempting to grapple with issues such as capabilities, there is a tendency to atomise its components rather than realise that its value is the interaction and iteration of its constituent elements. The value of capabilities, for instance, resides less in specific people than in more intangible issues of how they interact, co-operate and make decisions within their organisational context.[1]

To move away from product/market considerations, Figure 4.1 suggests internal areas and combinations to consider.

Fig. 4.1 **Potential structural, functional and process alignments**

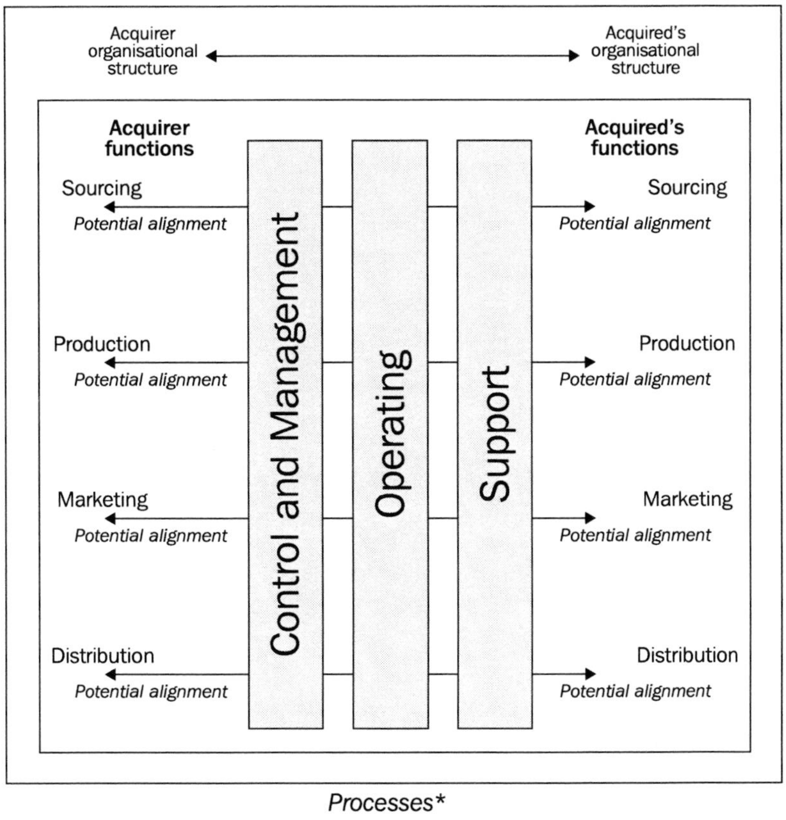

*Processes

Control and management processes	• Communications and information management • Financial controls • Legal issues • Reputational/ethical issues
Operating processes	• Customer management and service • Advertising and sales management process • Order fulfilment • Contracts management
Support processes	• Strategic and business planning • Human resource management • Technology management • Procurement process • New product/process/resource development

Key integration action plan

Consideration of the synergies and opportunities that need to be realised, the risks to be minimised, as well as the short-term taking charge actions, will lead to a series of integration issues that must be tackled. *All key integration issues for all areas* may be listed on a **key integration action plan** and an individual given named responsibility (see Figure 4.2). The key integration action plan should provide a complete and continuous guide to the state of integration actions.

Fig. 4.2 Key integration action plan

Integration issue*	Key actions	Individual responsible	Progress to date	Deadline for completion

* Some companies prefer to order these by function, business process, cognitive mapping processes etc.

From this key integration action plan, specific areas of initiative can be broken out in a hierarchy of attachments. These areas of initiative can be formatted in the same way.

Integration progress

To introduce a time element, a Gantt chart can be compiled to show major milestones in the process and provide comparisons of planned against actual progress. Figure 4.3 shows some of the main areas of integration that might appear where two manufacturing firms intend to bring production under one roof.

Fig. 4.3 Some key issues for integrating a manufacturing company

Chart date Acquisition date + 5 months **Milestones**														

Months													
	-3	-2	-1	1	2	3	4	5	6	7	8	9
	Due diligence		①	②		③	④		⑤			⑥

Milestones	Integration actions
	Broad plans
	Detailed plans
	Internal communication
	Transfer accounting functions
	Transfer contracts and other legal issues
	Transfer other head office functions
	Liaise with key customers
	Prioritise product transfers
	Ensure parent facilities ready to receive unit transfer
	Transfer stocks
	Transfer purchasing
	Transfer manufacturing
	Transfer product support
	Transfer hardware engineering
	Transfer software engineering
	Integrate information systems
	Integrate human resources

Acquisition date

Today's date

Milestones

① Detailed plan sign-off

② Finalise integration teams

③ Stocks move complete

④ Acquired head office closed down

⑤ Manufacturing and engineering transfer complete

⑥ Site cleared for sale

Key: Solid lines represent actual progress.
Dotted lines represent planned progress.

Within each area there will be considerable detail which can also be represented in the same way. For instance, for the human resources function, a Gantt chart might appear as follows:

Fig. 4.4 Gantt chart for some human resource issues

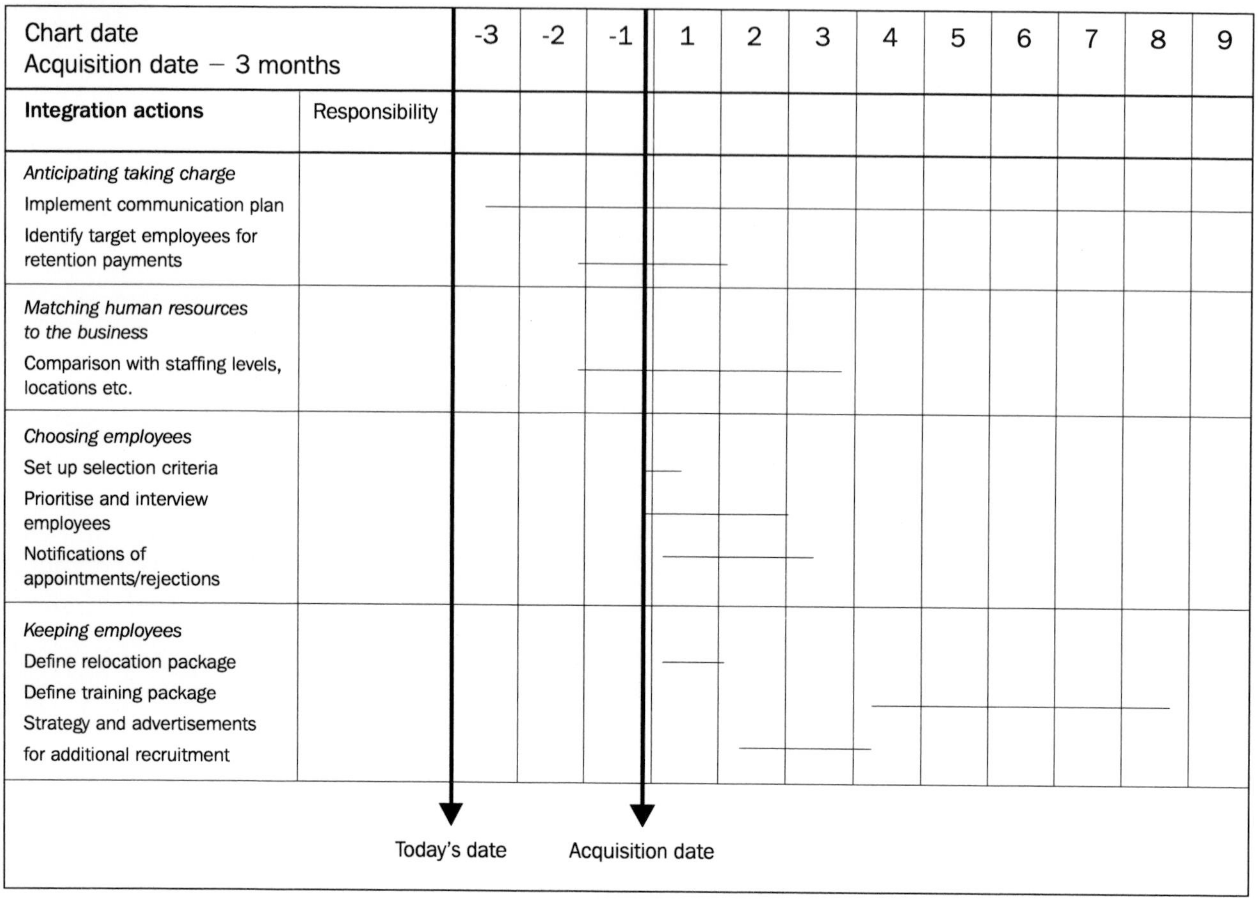

Chart date Acquisition date − 3 months		-3	-2	-1	1	2	3	4	5	6	7	8	9
Integration actions	Responsibility												
Anticipating taking charge Implement communication plan Identify target employees for retention payments													
Matching human resources to the business Comparison with staffing levels, locations etc.													
Choosing employees Set up selection criteria Prioritise and interview employees Notifications of appointments/rejections													
Keeping employees Define relocation package Define training package Strategy and advertisements for additional recruitment													

Today's date   Acquisition date

Gantt charts have excellent visual impact and so are good for communicating project plans as well as for day-to-day project control. However, they do have their limitations in that they can be overburdened with detail and then become too busy. Another potential limitation is that they are not very good at showing relationships between the different activities. For this reason, for more complex situations, the critical path method is useful.

Critical path method

The critical path method shows the logic of the relationship between activities in diagrammatic form. It highlights particularly important activities and the critical path shows the duration of the project. Beneath the network overview, there would be layers of sub-networks. As an example, Figure 4.5 shows a sub-network for an integration sequence for related human resource issues. The critical path is that with the lowest float times,[2] namely 1–5, 8, 10–13.

Fig. 4.5 The critical path for some human resource integration issues

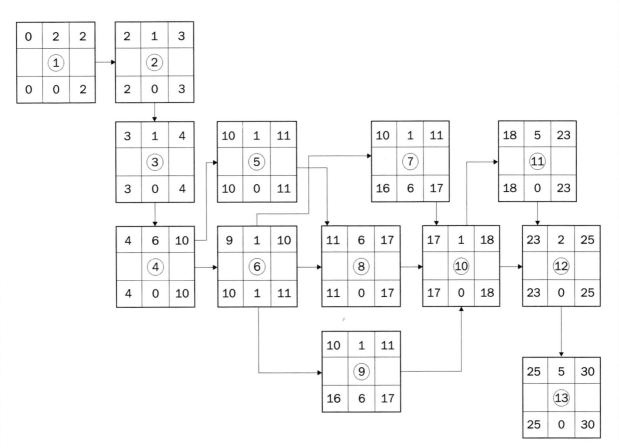

Matrix key

Earliest start time	Duration	Earliest finish time
	Activity number and description	
Latest start time	Total float	Latest finish time

Note: all figures are in months

Activity key

1. Set up employee communication plan
2. Define loyalty bonuses
3. Identify key target employees for loyalty bonuses
4. Compare staffing levels with business processes
5. Identify re-locations
6. Set up selection criteria
7. Set up relocation package
8. Prioritise and interview employees
9. Set up redundancy package
10. Notify employees of appointment or rejection
11. Advertise and interview external candidates
12. Employee acceptances
13. Begin orientation training

Source: Adapted from Slack, Chambers, Harland, Harrison, Johnston (1998). Reproduced by kind permission of the authors from Operations Management, 2nd edn., Pitman Publishing

Project management in uncertainty

Post-acquisition management can differ from conventional project management as:

■ the acquirer often has limited information with which to plan and yet needs to take action before a full picture is available;

■ the corporate configuration in which the project plan is originated may have very significant but hidden differences from the acquired company.

The acquirer may have to plan with limited information but will need to act, taking charge of the new acquisition, before full information becomes available. In some instances then, there will need to be a series of taking charge actions whilst information is being gathered for crystallising the medium-term plan. As this information becomes available, the acquirer may well need to adjust both short- and medium-term plans. However, should the taking charge phase be poorly handled, it is likely that there will need to be significant adjustments to expectations and even the overall strategic intent (see Figure 4.6).

Fig. 4.6 **A feedback model for taking charge of an acquisition**

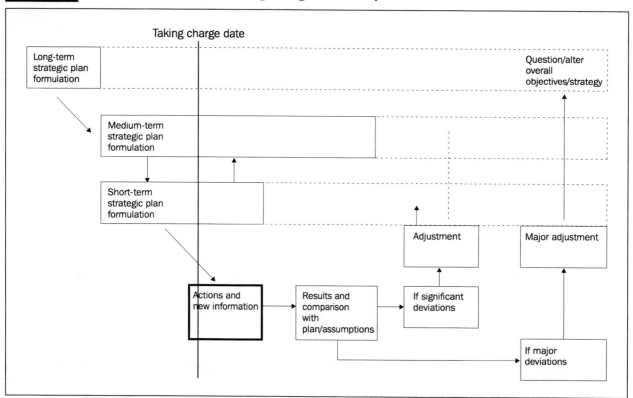

Source: Adapted from Grinyer and Spender (1979)

PRE-COMPLETION PREPARATION

After the deal has been signed and before the acquirer can take charge of the acquisition, there may be a window of opportunity. There may be opportunities to:

- establish deeper links between businesses to aid the integration process;
- consider using the exiting acquired CEO to help the integration process;
- set up integration teams.

Establish deeper links between businesses

Some acquirers already possess considerable knowledge about the target company. This may have arisen through close trading relationships, involvement in strategic alliances and joint ventures, ownership of shares in the target or a presence on the board. Nevertheless, where full integration of businesses is intended, it is important for there to be real depth in pre-acquisition discussions, both in content and in the range of managers involved from both companies.

The difficulty for senior managers is that, in grappling with 'the big picture', they can easily lose sight of details which then may become significant problems. To get beneath the surface of the various functions and processes, it is essential to allow opposite managers to speak to one another, to understand in practical terms how parts of the business may fit together and, as quickly as possible, to uncover major potential problems.

For regulatory reasons, in most public acquisitions before completion, such rich links are unlikely to occur except at the most senior level. However, some acquirers are able to broaden their understanding by arranging informal conversations between key, opposite managers.

In some instances, however, there is an opportunity for real dialogue before completion occurs. For instance, where the companies have agreed upon acquisition but now await formal clearance from the regulatory authorities, a great deal of useful preparatory work can be done. Some areas of the business may easily be damaged by a poor transition stage. In particular, managers from areas such as sales should be brought together to discuss how they will operate during the hand-over to avoid damaging the customer base. Other areas may not be so sensitive to immediate change in ownership, but may represent very significant core competencies of the organisations. If full integration is to occur in such areas, poor handling could easily damage capabilities which have taken years to create and may be very hard to repair. For instance, whilst on paper synergies between R&D departments may appear straightforward, meetings between opposite managers in these functions may reveal very substantial cultural differences. As Sir Richard Sykes was reported as saying to MPs, whilst speaking of the failed SmithKline Beecham/Glaxo merger,

> *the scientists who represent the intellectual capital of drug companies are 'a lot of sensitive flowers' who are quite able to walk out if upset. (Durman, 1998, The Times, 23 April)*

Replacing such high-quality scientists might have been a very difficult task.

Involving key employees in the acquired company also has a further value in that they feel involved in the process and may have an influence upon their future. Bringing together the acquirers and their opposite numbers helps to build trust and confidence and, importantly, gives 'the enemy' a face.

The importance acquirers place upon reducing uncertainty is shown by the growing trend for acquirers to hold away-days for opposite managers in key functions. Where it is critical to retain target company employees, retention bonuses will be offered, as is currently common in the Information Technology industry, and there may also be social events for both sets of managers and partners to get to know each other.

Consider using the exiting acquired CEO to help transition

If the CEO of the acquired company intends to leave the company after acquisition, perhaps through retirement, or a wish to pursue other interests, then provided that the acquirer regards him as trustworthy and he has run his business well, there is a strong case for seeking to retain him whilst the acquisition beds down.

The acquired CEO provides continuity for his employees and customers, so that there is no vacuum at the top. From his involvement in the negotiations he will have established a direct relationship with the acquirer's top managers and will be clear on their plans for the future. His greatest value will be interpreting those intentions in a way that makes sense for his organisation and his employees. Through his established leadership and, critically, his informal network, he will be able to bring about changes more smoothly and rapidly than the acquirer. Unlike a new CEO from outside the acquired company, who faces a double hurdle of having to learn about the business as well as build bridges to bring things about, the acquired CEO already understands how to make things happen. Apart from experiencing less resistance to change, the acquired CEO may also be able to suggest useful modifications to the acquirer's plans, stemming from his greater knowledge of what would work in his business. He is also likely to be able to avoid difficulties which an Outsider would not perceive.

To retain an acquired CEO it is possible to use earn-outs and other forms of financial incentive. Where the inducement is linked to the acquired company's performance, there is always a risk that the CEO would run the acquisition for short-term gain, which would not be in the parent company's best interests. If the acquired CEO is the founder of the business or has been CEO for a reasonably long time, it is more than likely that he will have a strong emotional attachment to his achievements with the company and its workforce. For this reason, he is likely to want to see the business prosper under new ownership and may well be happy to assist in helping the integration. In addition, he may also welcome the time to seek his next assignment.

There is a downside to retaining an acquired CEO. Where the acquired CEO is the founder of the business, he will tend to run the company in a similar way to before and will probably resist major changes which may alter or, in his eyes, damage that business's identity. Where the acquirer intends profound change which would re-configure the acquired company, or indeed disaggregate it, the retention of the acquired CEO would be most likely to present a very significant obstacle to change. Where the acquirer intends to change the very essence of the acquired company, the acquired CEO is likely to be more of a hindrance than a help.

The exception to this rule of letting go an acquired CEO when fundamental change is planned for his company is when the acquired CEO is widely perceived to have exceptionally broad management experience and industry expertise. This may be a very significant asset for the acquirer in 'group' terms. In this case, the acquirer would do well to attempt to promote this executive up into the group and distance him from his previous role.

Set up integration teams

Where a significant amount of post-acquisition change is envisaged, then the use of integration teams will be vital. These should be set up in essence, well before completion, so that they are ready to act as soon as the target is acquired. However, depending upon the style of integration intended, it may be important to give executives in the acquired company a major role. If significant interaction between the companies is possible before taking charge, then the membership of the main integration teams can be settled. If this is not possible, then establishing the membership of these teams will be a major priority immediately upon acquisition. As the latter is most likely to be the case, integration teams will be discussed more fully on p.87.

TAKING CHARGE

Taking charge[3] is a brief burst of activity which establishes that the world has changed for the acquired company.[4] Many see the handling of this burst of activity as critical to the success of the acquisition. For this reason a number of articles speak in terms of *'the first 90 days'* (Angwin and Ernst and Young, 1996), and the *'first 100 days'* (Hsieh and Bear, 1996; Hubbard, 1999: 17). Clear, positive and rapid handling of the acquired company is vital in the very early stages of post-acquisition ownership.

Speed

The driving message is that *taking charge* happens rapidly and has a definable end. It is a short period of fluidity, where previous practices and relationships falter, and should be used to advantage. As we have stressed above, this burst of activity requires considerable co-ordination and cannot be achieved effectively without advance planning – *'day one of ownership is too late!'*

The importance of rapid action when taking charge has led some consultants to recommend speed throughout the entire post-acquisition process. Coopers and Lybrand (1996), in their survey, *Speed makes the difference*, of 124 companies that had executed a merger or acquisition in the past three years, suggest that fast transitioning companies reported favourable performance much more often than slow transitioning companies, in terms of gross margin, productivity, profitability, · cash flow and speed to market. In *Five Frogs on a Log* (Feldman and Spratt 1999), partners of PricewaterhouseCooper's global M&A consulting division also strongly advocate speed of action throughout the post-acquisition process.

Whilst we concur that speed of action is important in taking charge of an acquisition, as inaction rapidly brings negative outcomes, beyond the taking charge phase we cannot make the same general recommendation. The type of integration style chosen should determine the pace of action as the author is well aware of many acquirers who *'acted in haste and are repenting at leisure'*. Clearly, as time is money, doing things more quickly should result in more rapid returns and senior managers will not want to take more time than necessary. However, it is important that speed of action is determined by the most appropriate process rather than the process being determined by what can be done rapidly. For instance, the value of the acquisition may be in learning from acquired employees, which requires trust and dialogue. However, rationalising facilities, which can be carried out rapidly, can completely undermine the more important purpose of the acquisition as key employees feel threatened and leave. Greater priority for rapid actions, then, may sacrifice the real purpose of the acquisition on the 'altar of speed'.

We are cautious therefore about the suggestion that speed is the key in all circumstances. After the taking charge phase, we can only suggest that managers act at a speed appropriate to their chosen style of integration. We shall return to the issue of speed in the next chapter.

Uncertainty

Stakeholders in the acquired company, particularly the employees, will be facing considerable uncertainty upon acquisition. Customers may wonder whether they can rely upon their supplier, or may find themselves more susceptible to the advances of competitors. For acquired employees, the psychological shock wave leads to anxiety and stress, which can rapidly result in dysfunctional behaviour. At the same time the new parent needs to understand fully what it has purchased and begin the integration process.

Stabilise the acquisition

The potential conflicts and uncertainty upon taking charge mean that it is essential for the new parent to *stabilise* the acquired company. This can be achieved by establishing:

1 An **interface management team** – to direct and control interactions between both companies.

2 **Clear leadership and vision** – to provide short-term direction quickly and restore the deeper sense of purpose in employees. This aims to restore/renew the psychological contract and frame employees' expectations.

3 **Excellent communications** – the method by which expectations are managed and change understood and orchestrated. Channels will be both formal and informal, with a variety of avenues for communication in each.

4 **Business evaluation and control** – to reveal what has really been purchased, allow adjustments to plans and assumptions, and prompt the co-ordination of management systems.

5 **Evidence of commitment** – small, concrete gestures can have major positive effects upon employees' morale. Employees will see such gestures as evidence that their expectations are grounded.

6 **Mutual cultural awareness and the foundations for change** – to avoid the worst problems of culture clash and begin to build a coherent group.

7 **Integration teams** – to facilitate cultural and organisational integration.

All of these actions need to occur *at the same time*. However, it is clear that some aspects of these actions are about the acquirer taking charge, understanding the acquisition and putting in place mechanisms for managing it, whilst other aspects are about managing employees' concerns so that they are motivated to make the acquisition work and not minded to act in ways which might be destabilising. The attitude of employees towards this tension will be formed by the gap between their expectations and the changes and actions they see around them.

It is vital that the acquirer recognises that employees form expectations rapidly and that the 'stakes' for not matching these expectations, for instance by going back on promises, is 'trust' in top management. If trust is eroded, a manager's credibility suffers, and employees' morale and motivation deteriorate. This may well harm the integration and will become a barrier to companies attempting to build mutual understanding and credibility. The acquirer therefore needs to manage employees' expectations through the categories set out above, recognising that these are interlinked. For instance, good communications without consistency of action, or action where the logic is not communicated (Hubbard, 1999), will serve to undermine trust in management.

This does not mean that companies should allow the taking charge phase to drift on unchecked, as newness is a depreciating asset. There is an expectation of change which diminishes over time. The longer it takes to take charge, the more 'frozen' the acquisition will become as 'the will for change' ebbs and resistance to change grows. In other words, seize the initiative, frame expectations and have a defined set of outcomes.

We shall now look in some detail at each of the seven stages we have listed as being essential for stabilising the acquisition.

Interface management team

The importance of interface management is to protect the acquired company from the activities of the parent. The 'conquering hero' syndrome can be very destructive of the acquired company's competencies as over-zealous managers from the acquirer rush to shape the new acquisition in their own image. By establishing interface management, a series of filters and controls can be used to influence the extent and speed of the integration process. This should help protect the value in the acquired company as well as allow necessary changes. The importance and extent of this filtering will depend upon the post-acquisition integration style (see Chapter 5).

Interface management should be headed by the executive managing the acquired company. Should this executive come from the acquirer, then it will also be critical to have a senior executive from the acquired company. There will also need to be support staff. There is significant value in this team being located away from the parent company. The interface team needs to filter out or restrict the number of demands from the parent as well as to restrict the channels through which demands are fed (Haspeslagh and Jemison, 1991).

The penalty for not setting up interface management is that demands which may seem reasonable to the parent company will be perceived by the acquired company as an avalanche of costly, unrealistic impositions. In trying to satisfy these demands, the acquired company can falter under the administrative burden and the demands may also tear unwittingly at the fabric of the company itself.

This problem can be particularly damaging when the acquired company is much smaller than the parent and may not have the same amount of support staff. It is likely to be very damaging if there are significant differences between the businesses which are not fully appreciated by the new parent.

Clear leadership and vision

The purpose of a clear vision is to give employees a new confidence in the organisation and trust in the management of the new group. The acquired company's employees need to be reinvigorated after acquisition and need to reaffirm their commitment to the organisation. The vision should help them achieve this deep motivation, provided it is translated into a credible mission statement that has real meaning to them. If it is too vague, it will serve no purpose. If it makes promises which cannot be met, trust and credibility will be undermined.

In some instances, it may not be possible to give a clear answer as to where the organisation is going. In order to build trust and credibility, it is better to be honest about this and to say that a vision is being developed, and support this general message with suitable actions.

An example of a post-merger vision is *'the promise of SmithKline Beecham'* (see Figure 4.7).

Fig. 4.7 A vision statement

*'the purpose of our merger is to build a **new**[5] and better healthcare company. "New" in the sense of being well prepared for the future . . . as a global competitor; "better" in that, from the strengths and traditions of **both**[6] companies, we seek to build SmithKline Beecham as a company that sets standards for the industry.'*

Source: Bauman, Jackson, Lawrence (1997)

'The promise set out the new company's definition of winning and its commitment to becoming the best, not only in terms of financial performance, but also in terms of the kind of company SB hoped to be. More than a vision, the word "promise" implied commitment' (Bauman, Jackson, Lawrence, 1997).

Excellent communications

Uncertainty is damaging, so excellent communications, designed to reduce or remove it, are vital for successful post-acquisition management. For this reason, when it comes to stating the importance of communication, *'Communicate, communicate, communicate!'*.

The choice of communication medium affects the meaning of the message. Where there is complexity and unfamiliarity with the situation, effective communication requires media richness. This is achieved by an intensive, interactive style of communication through a broad range of delivery channels. By these means, the aims of good post-acquisition communication are to:

■ convey a clear message;

■ be able to handle multiple information cues simultaneously;

■ allow and enable rapid feedback;

■ establish a personal focus.

Source: Lengel and Daft (1988)

Communication, through a variety of delivery mechanisms, needs to be continuous throughout the post-acquisition process, and be able to penetrate right down to the very bottom of the organisation.

> *Companies that communicated early and frequently about plans, objectives and progress reported smoother transitions and more immediate results. (Coopers and Lybrand, 1996)*

Internal communications

The purpose of internal communications is to manage employees' concerns and frame expectations by:

■ gaining managers' and employees' buy-in to the acquirer's vision and its implications;

■ countering personal shock waves;

■ neutralising uncertainty.

Early communications to employees should address the following issues contained in Figure 4.8.

It is important, as always, to avoid tokenism here, as content-free or highly generalised messages will not achieve the desired ends. Likewise, false promises will quickly be found out and negative effects follow as trust in top management is eroded.

Fig. 4.8 Early framing of employee expectations and reducing concerns

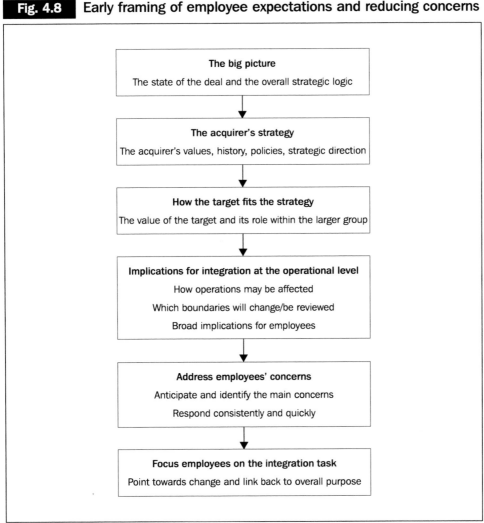

Many communication avenues are open to the acquirer in different types of media. These are shown in Figure 4.9.

Fig. 4.9 Internal communications matrix

	Personal meeting	Video telephone	Telephone	Team meetings	Personal E-mail	Personal letter	General event	Intranet	General video	Special booklet	Special newsletter	Normal newsletter
Top management												
Senior managers												
Other employees												
Retired employees												

Increasing richness[7]

The internal communications matrix is only indicative of the possibilities. The quality and degree of communication saturation needed will reflect:

- the shock of the acquisition;
- the amount of change intended;
- the number and distribution of employees;
- the extent to which the acquirer wishes to retain employees;[8]
- the opportunities for employees to leave.

It is also useful to have a question and answer mechanism which will remove the feeling of powerlessness among employees by addressing their main fears. The best form would be in face-to-face meetings, but for large acquisitions this is not possible. Some acquirers have set up dedicated telephone hot-lines for rapid, up to date, personal interaction. Others have used question boxes to give employees the opportunity to voice their opinions and concerns, and bulletins to respond, on a company-wide basis, to the most common enquiries. The recent use of intranets seems to be popular, provided they are updated at appropriate times, as they allow employees access to immediate developments at times convenient to them.

The general advice regarding communication is that:

- it is better to over- than under-communicate;
- several modes of delivery are more effective than relying on just one or two;
- communications need to penetrate right down into the organisation and not *'stop at the outer door of headquarters' inner sanctum'* (Kesner and Fowler, 1997);
- communications need to be continuous, with real, relevant content;
- the message must be reliable and honest.

The importance of communication is exemplified by the case of a merger between two management consultancies, where retaining skilled employees was of paramount importance. The consultants were well respected in the marketplace and would have had little trouble in finding other employment. This is illustrated by the comments of the CEO.

Keeping the key people – that was the issue. People have to feel motivated to what you do. Unless you take the trouble to communicate to them properly, steadily, you can't win in a business like this. You have to, to some extent, take the people along with you. Even if they don't agree with what you're doing, you have to persuade them that you're doing it with the right intent.

As a result, there was a high density of communications. Before the deal was announced, they produced documents so that employees would not face an information vacuum.

> *Firstly we produced a carefully, carefully written document to make sure everyone in the organisation very quickly got something in their hand that had our message, before they invented their own. That was in the post at the same time as the announcement hit the stock exchange screen.*

Once the announcement had been made, the CEO embarked on rapid, high impact communication to guide employees and remove uncertainty.

> *On this particular occasion we felt it was the people at the top who had to talk to everybody, or as close as possible to everybody, trying to soothe the obvious anxieties. We couldn't announce the meetings until the deal was in the public domain. Between the announcement and the consummation, over a period of three days, I visited every single office of both consultancies in the UK and spoke to about 50% of staff. We got to another 30% during the following three weeks. I then got to all the overseas offices as well, and we talked on the phone to them in advance. It was a major exercise.*

For larger deals, such as the SmithKline Beecham (SKB) merger, the issue of a core message and the alignment of management and employees remained critical. To ensure one corporate-wide voice and yet have high, meaningful impact at the local level, SKB agreed on the core message, processes and media centrally, but then delivered locally through management. This allowed local accents in the dissemination of the message, and it was important for employees to perceive how the message was linked to local business performance (Bauman, Jackson, Lawrence, 1997).

External communications

The purpose of Figure 4.10 is less to indicate what forms of communication will be mandatory, owing to the demands of the stock exchange requirements for instance, than to demonstrate what other possibilities exist and should be considered in the very short period just before the announcement date.[9]

Fig. 4.10 **External communications matrix – the announcement window**

	Press release	Advertise-ment	Special booklet	Internet web site	Special event	Promotional item	Video	Special newsletter	Personal meeting	Personal letter	E-mail
Major customers											
Major suppliers											
Banks											
Institutional shareholders											
Key investors											
Shareholders											
City analysts											
Financial media											
National media											
Local media											
Directories											
General public											
Pressure groups											
Local authorities											
Regulatory authorities											

Figure 4.11 shows the possibilities for communicating with external stakeholders during the post-acquisition phase. It will be sufficient to brief some stakeholders at the outset of the post-acquisition phase. Others will need a much longer dialogue. Assuming that the stakeholders are interested in how the post-acquisition phase shapes up, the quality and timing of updates will be determined by the level of stakeholder power and the durability of the message. For instance, with a key customer, considerable efforts may be needed up front for their assurance and to retain contracts, but then their interest may subside for some time. The media may have an even shorter time horizon and require much more intense updating and then lose interest.

Fig. 4.11 External communications matrix – the post-acquisition phase

	Advertise-ment	Special booklet	Internet web site	Special event	Promotional item	Video	Magazine article	Special newsletter	Personal meeting	Corporate letter	Personal letter	E-mail
Retail customers												
Commercial customers												
Raw material suppliers												
Banks												
Institutional shareholders												
Key investors												
Shareholders												
City analysts												
Financial media												
National media												
Local media												
General public												
Pressure groups												
Local authorities												
Regulatory authorities												

Communications programme

Figure 4.12 is a generalised illustration of a communications programme.

Fig. 4.12 Communications programme

AD* - 2 weeks	AD - 1 week	AD - 2 days
• Agree post-acquisition communication message amongst directors	• Confirm communication distribution list	• Finish press release
• Set up and print special booklets	• Finalise announcement day presentation to employees	
• Set up acquisition page on web site/intranet	• Record video	

	AD - 2 days
	• Post letter and booklet about the acquisition to all employees
	• Notify employees of meetings
	• Speak with distributors

Announcement day	AD + 2 days	Pre-closing	Post-closing
• Press conference	• Begin visits to offices, factories	• Combined management meetings	• Regular newsletter
• Contact key customers			• Bulletin updates
• Contact key suppliers		• Set up and brief joint integration teams	• Orientation seminars

• At acquired company head office:
  – meetings for senior employees
  – presentations to other employees
		• Newsletter	• Regular web site updates

			• Weekly team meetings
• Update web site/intranet			• Harmonise companies' communications

* AD = Announcement date

Establishing business evaluation and control

Business evaluation

Throughout the negotiations, even friendly ones, the acquiree will be trying to present his company in the best light. It is important for acquirers to review the situation immediately after completion, to assure themselves that their assumptions and risk assessments are accurate. Although the need for this will relate to the quality of pre-acquisition due diligence, the level of pre-acquisition access to the acquired company and the way in which the acquired company is to be integrated, Chapter 2 has already shown how pre-acquisition enquiries can be limited to the harder elements and understate important soft factors.

If the acquirer has been fortunate in gaining very significant access to the acquisition and its employees before completion, they may need just a series of informal discussions with key managers to check upon key areas of business risk and verify cultural issues and other core assumptions. Provided that there is a level of trust between the parties, now that they are 'all in the same ship', the acquirer needs to see whether the acquired managers feel there are any details which may have been 'overlooked' and could affect assumptions behind the pre-acquisition integration plans.

In other circumstances, such as hostile take-overs, or take-overs that have to be completed very rapidly, there may need to be a full-blown post-acquisition audit. In particular, even though many of the uncertainties thrown up by the pre-acquisition due diligence will have been warranted, acquirers should satisfy themselves of the real extent of risks: it is little consolation to know that you may win a legal action some years in the future whilst the business collapses in the present. It is vital to be fully aware of cultural differences.

One way to embark on establishing what has been bought is to construct a post-acquisition integration plan. Integration teams can be used to gather data, verify pre-acquisition assumptions, refine details, improve levels of understanding and provide recommendations. The post-acquisition integration plan can then be compared against pre-acquisition expectations.

As shown in Chapter 2, the costs involved in possessing an inaccurate view of the acquired company can be considerable, leading to an inability to generate the synergies expected and, ultimately, to the sale of the acquisition at a greatly reduced price.

Control

For the parent to understand the acquisition and to aid reporting, it is important to harmonise accounting systems. In the words of one CEO in the Information Technology business, *'You don't really know what you've got until you've expressed it through your own systems'*. In practice, the parent control systems almost always come to prevail over acquired company practices. A report by Business International (1992: 71) states that: *'There seemed to be no question that the control system of the acquirer had to be adopted'*.

Acquirers should avoid imposing an entire control system at the outset and refrain from imposing a big company system onto a small company. This will only lead to the latter being buried under demands, spending more time form filling than operating the business. In line with the spirit of setting up interface management, begin with the essentials, the finance area, and practise restraint.

For many acquirers sending in finance teams is a first and most important step: *'They are the shock troops of the acquisition, charged with gaining control of cash, other liquid assets and the financial reporting system'* (McCann and Gilkey, 1988: 155). Whilst most acquired managing executives complain about the onerous nature of the reporting procedures, many begrudgingly acknowledge that these procedures of the acquirer are superior to their own.

In his study of Management Accounting Techniques (MATs), Jones (1985a) examined their use in 30 quoted companies. Figure 4.13 shows the most important techniques used at the time of acquisition and after two years.

Fig. 4.13 Main Management Accounting Techniques post-acquisition

Rank	At the time of acquisition	Two years after acquisition
1.	Cost/profit centre control	Monthly accounts and reports
2.	Budgeting in operating companies	Budgeting in operating companies
3.	Variance reports in companies	Formalised capital expenditure appraisal and control
4.	Monthly accounts and reports	Delegated authority for capital expenditure
5.	Participative budget setting in companies	Participative budget setting in companies
6.	Formalised capital expenditure appraisal and control	Cost/profit centre control
7.	Delegated authority for capital expenditure	Variance reports in companies
8.	Marginal costing for decision making	Marginal costing for decision making
9.	Weekly cash flow reports	Long-range planning
10.	Long-range planning	Strategic planning

Source: Adapted from Jones (1985a: 183)

Jones (1985a) observed that integration was achieved by modifying well accepted MATs rather than by introducing unique systems. Importantly, his study examined a range of different acquisition types and discovered remarkable similarities between them, suggesting that *'acquirers were not discriminating in the changes made to MATs'* (Jones, 1985a) and that there was *'a substantial degree of carry over from one organisation to another, regardless of organisational differences'* (Jones, 1985b: 321).

As a whole, Jones (1985a) observed that MATs assumed greater importance during the years following acquisition[10] than at other times. In particular we can see from Figure 4.14 that the techniques identified by Jones (1985) as having the greatest overall importance in the post-acquisition phase, namely monthly accounts and reports, budgeting in operating companies and formalised capital expenditure, have a wide range of influence. This suggests that MATs are not used just for control but are *'a force for organisational change'* (Wilson, 1992: 65).

Fig. 4.14 Most important Management Accounting Techniques and their areas of influence

Areas influenced by MATs	Organisational	Integration	Motivation			Decision making		Performance measurement
Enabling characteristics	Delegated authority	Communication of objectives	Participation	Level of budget	Feedback/ interpretation of results	Contribution to problem solving – long term	Contribution to problem solving – short term	Performance measurement
Monthly accounts					✓		✓	✓
Budgets in operating companies	✓	✓	✓	✓			✓	
Formalised capital expenditure		✓			✓	✓		✓

Source: Adapted from Jones (1985a)

Evidence of commitment

Actions speak louder than words. The extent to which the acquirer wishes to support the acquired company in its current form will vary depending upon the intended integration approach. However, there are likely to be some weaknesses in the acquired company that need to be addressed to restore the acquisition's stability. These may involve modest expenditure and the bringing in of expertise. Whilst these actions will aid the business, they can have a very powerful symbolic effect.

When taking charge of a substantial acquisition in the food industry, the acquirer found the main office building to be in a dreadful state; the previous owners not seeing why they should invest in it if they were about to exit. The acquirer immediately carried out renovations. Upon reflection, the acquiring managing executive remarked:

> *In terms of early signals, you can reap multiples of the small investment you make. It was a big sign. It didn't cost a fortune, but I reckon I would have spent five times that looking back, because it was a very, very important signal.*

Commitment does not just have to be in expenditure. One extraordinary example from a merger of multinationals was when a senior member of the acquirer's management team attended the funeral of one of the acquired company manager's close relatives. This representation from the new parent company showed a commitment that was widely appreciated and commented upon in the acquired company.

Small concrete actions can have a major positive effect upon employees' morale.

Establishing cultural awareness and laying foundations for change

As shown in Chapter 2, even in apparently similar businesses, there may be profound cultural differences, which can erode the quality of the post-acquisition process. However, essential difficulty with corporate cultures is that they are largely submerged from view. The clues tend to be minor, but conceal substantial obstacles to change. Most employees are unaware of the actual underpinnings of their corporate culture which will include national and regional elements and industry/sector influences, all bound up in the organisation's history. Employees will tend only to recognise superficial representations such as corporate brochures, logos, signs of rank such as parking slots, office furniture, and meal arrangements. However, these are pawns in what can be a larger cultural conflict. The difficulty comes, therefore, when an acquirer alters some of these visible signs. To the acquirer his actions may seem to be minor, although will probably be driven by his own submerged set of values and beliefs. The item to be changed may be minor in the context of the operation of the business, but may represent something far more fundamental. For this reason, apparently insignificant issues, such as taking coffee breaks, may suddenly assume much greater importance than the acquirer expected. The culture iceberg becomes apparent.

Where cultural integration is intended, culture can be surfaced by a variety of methods from remote postal questionnaires to personal or group meetings between employees and facilitators. Often 'cultural workouts' are organised, where focus groups create a map of the acquirer's culture relative to the acquirer's and identify actions for bridging gaps, such as two-way employee exchanges, tuition in the different culture and other socialisation programmes. The general aims are:

- creating cultural awareness
- clarifying company cultures
- promoting mutual respect.

National and regional cultures

When we speak of cultural differences, we tend to think immediately of differences at the national level. Visual and auditory cues are most immediate in terms of language and appearance. However these are surface manifestations of differences in attitudes, perceptions and understandings which run at a much deeper level. Hofstede (1993) has exposed these fundamental differences with his five dimensions for understanding national culture characteristics.

1 Power distance – the degree of inequality amongst people

2 Individualism – the extent to which people prefer to act as individuals rather than as members of groups

3 Masculinity – the extent to which tough values, such as assertiveness, performance, competition, prevail over tender values such as quality of life, maintaining warm relationships, care for the weak, service

4 Uncertainty avoidance – the degree to which people in a country prefer structured over unstructured situations

5 Long term orientation – long term would-be values oriented to the future in terms of saving, persistence, whereas short term would find values oriented to the past and present such as respect for tradition and fulfilling social obligation.

Hofstede's dimensions expose striking differences between National cultures and can give useful insights to cross border acquisitions. For instance some of the difficulties highlighted earlier in Chapter 2 page 29 in the Pharmacia of Sweden and Upjohn of America merger, can be attributed to such core cultural differences. For instance, the frictions between management styles is less surprising when viewed through Hofstede's framework, and may have been managed differently.

Hofstede's work has been extended by Trompenaars and Hampden-Turner (1999) who offer their own set of National cultural dimensions. In particular they view these dimensions as dilemmas to be resolved and suggest ten steps to achieve this reconciliation.

1　The theory of complementarity

2　Using humour

3　Mapping out a cultural space

4　From nouns to present participles and processes

5　Language and meta–language

6　Frames and context

7　Sequencing

8　Waving/cycling

9　Synergising and virtuous circling

10　The double helix

Source: Trompenaars and Hampden-Turner (1999: 200)

To show how these steps may be helpful, one of the dimensions identified by Trompenaars and Hampden-Turner is Universalist versus Particularist: the former approach is that 'what is good and right can be defined and always applies' (Trompenaars and Hampden-Turner 1999 : 8) whereas the latter approach gives greater attention to the obligations of relationships and unique circumstances. Examples of national differences on this dimension might be the USA as a Universalist culture, relying on the law to protect the truth, and Venezuela where friendships have special obligations and may come above the law. The former would probably regard the latter as corrupt, the latter would be suspicious of the honesty of the former's institutions. To reconcile this dilemma, Trompenaars and Hampden-Turner remind us that these cultural positions:

1 are holistic and therefore complementary

2 humour will signal unexpected clashes and reveal the real dilemmas

3 can be considered as two axes and so form a cultural space, allowing a clearer definition of what has to be achieved

4 can be perceived as processes – Universalising and Particularising

5 can occupy different levels of abstraction, so that 'Universal' is the general rule of operation under which 'Particular' can operate, or vice versa

6 may not need to be expressed simultaneously, and a sequence may avoid conflict

7 may be viewed as a wave form, with behaviours oscillating between the two positions by means of an error correction system.

By melding the two cultures, a virtuous circle should be achieved, allowing synergy. In this example a company might aim for rules that encompass ever more particulars.

Regional Culture is also worth mentioning although to the best of the author's knowledge, regional cultural differences in mergers and acquisitions have not been studied. In countries as large as the USA, variations in attitude to business practice are clearly apparent and yet often ignored. As Disney discovered, in its $19bn acquisition of Capital Cities/ABC in 1995, there were huge cultural and geographic problems in moving a New York based business to Los Angeles (*The Economist*, 11–17 September 1999). In smaller countries, regional differences can still be very pronounced. The author is aware of a number of acquisitions where employees would not move surprisingly small distances of 20 to 30 miles as it would take them into a different region. In Scotland for instance a number of acquirers have found difficulties in moving employees between Edinburgh and Glasgow, and experienced different attitudes to business. Other European countries such as France may have even greater claims to significant regional variation. Pluralism has been generally accepted as a national characteristic in

France and this may be a reflection of the existing diversity amongst its regions. The 'joke' of what is a typical Frenchman has prompted the eminent historian, Theodore Zeldin (1993) to write a highly acclaimed work which seeks to identify whether there is something definable as 'The French'.

Organisational culture

The strategy and values of an organisation may be written down, but to understand the real culture of an organisation, the assumptions need to be surfaced. The analytical frameworks to tackle organisational culture vary in terms of scope and orientation. Some present holistic pictures of organisational configuration, such as the popular McKinsey 7-S framework, which powerfully demonstrates the importance of interaction between components, whilst others adopt a much narrower focus, emphasising mainly behavioural characteristics. A useful broad framework which can be used to analyse and compare organisational cultures is the cultural web (see Figure 4.15).

Fig. 4.15 The cultural web

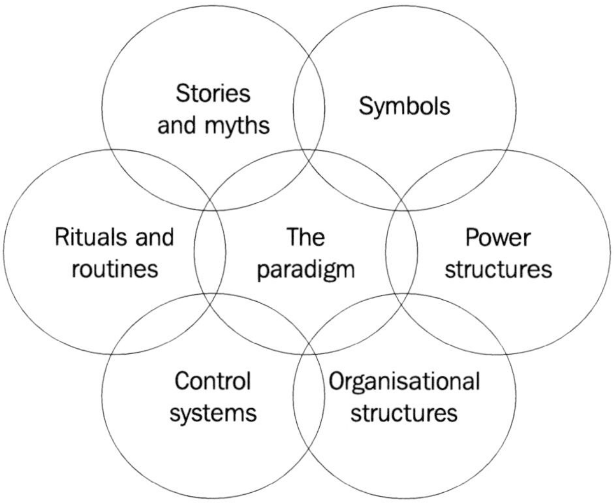

Source: Johnson and Scholes (1999: 74). Reproduced with the kind permission of the authors from *Exploring Corporate Strategy*, 5th Edition, Pearson Education Ltd, Prentice Hall Europe.

Organisational culture can be thought of as a series of layers, with the outer and most visible layer being the carefully presented public face contained in annual reports, press releases, business plans. Whilst this may be a true reflection of the intentions of the company, it may give a misleading impression of how the culture of the company exists in the minds and hearts of the people within and around the organisation. The inner layer, or 'real' culture, is in the way the organisation actually operates: *'It is the taken for granted assumptions about "how you run an organisation like this" and "what really matters around here"'* (Johnson and Scholes, 1999: 236). These elements can be surfaced by listening to day-to-day conversation, having discussions, and through observation of what people take for granted. These findings can then be linked to political, symbolic and structural aspects of the organisation.

The sorts of questions that can be asked to surface the real culture are shown in Figure 4.16.

Fig. 4.16 **Questions to surface real culture**

Stories
- What core beliefs do stories reflect?
- How pervasive are these beliefs (through levels)?
- Do stories relate to
  - strengths or weaknesses?
  - successes or failures?
  - conformity or mavericks?
- Who are the heroes and villains?
- What norms do the mavericks deviate from?

Routines and rituals
- Which routines are emphasised?
- Which would look odd if changed?
- What behaviour do routines encourage?
- What are the key rituals?
- What core beliefs do they reflect?
- What do training programmes emphasise?
- How easy are rituals/routines to change?

Organisational structure
- How mechanistic/organic are the structures?
- How flat/hierarchical are the structures?
- How formal/informal are the structures?
- Do structures encourage collaboration or competition?
- What type of power structure do they support?

Control systems
- What is most closely monitored/controlled?
- Is emphasis on reward or punishment?
- Are controls related to history or current strategies?
- Are there many/few controls?

Power structures
- What are the core beliefs of the leadership?
- How strongly held are these beliefs (idealists or pragmatists)?
- How is power distributed in the organisation?
- Where are the main blockages to change?

Continued

Symbols
- What language and jargon is used?
- How internal or accessible is it?
- What aspects of strategy are highlighted in publicity?
- What status symbols are there?
- Are there particular symbols which denote the organisation?

Overall
- What is the dominant culture (defender, prospector, analyser)?
- How easy is this to change?

Source: Johnson and Scholes (1999: 238). Reproduced with the kind permission of the authors from *Exploring Corporate Strategy*, 5th Edition, Pearson Education Ltd, Prentice Hall Europe.

It is unlikely that an entire organisational culture can be characterised as one type of culture, as there are likely to be sub-cultures. However, the key issue is to expose differences between sub-cultures that are likely to be integrated. The critical factor to remember with such frameworks, however, is that they are interlocking and self-reinforcing. In other words, changing just one aspect will not produce cultural change, as the other elements will work to restore the status quo.

Cultural profiles

Another and popular way of illustrating cultural differences is by cultural profiles. This involves counterposing assessments for each company by key cultural issues. This form of display clearly illustrates similarities and differences in cultural emphasis.

An example of two fictitious companies is given in Figure 4.17.

From Figure 4.17 it is clear that the companies exhibit very different cultural profiles. If the intention is to change the acquired company in order to reflect the parent's culture, there will be very considerable obstacles, not least the loss of individual autonomy.

Fig. 4.17 Cultural profiling

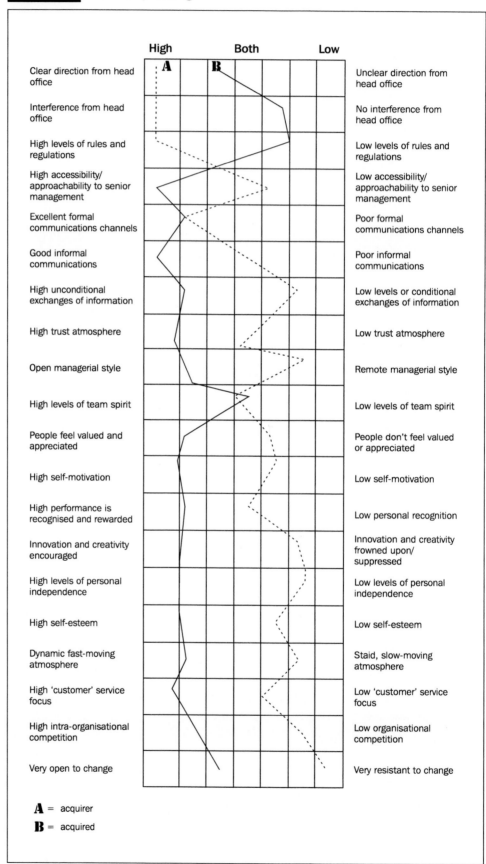

	High	Both	Low	
Clear direction from head office				Unclear direction from head office
Interference from head office				No interference from head office
High levels of rules and regulations				Low levels of rules and regulations
High accessibility/ approachability to senior management				Low accessibility/ approachability to senior management
Excellent formal communications channels				Poor formal communications channels
Good informal communications				Poor informal communications
High unconditional exchanges of information				Low levels or conditional exchanges of information
High trust atmosphere				Low trust atmosphere
Open managerial style				Remote managerial style
High levels of team spirit				Low levels of team spirit
People feel valued and appreciated				People don't feel valued or appreciated
High self-motivation				Low self-motivation
High performance is recognised and rewarded				Low personal recognition
Innovation and creativity encouraged				Innovation and creativity frowned upon/ suppressed
High levels of personal independence				Low levels of personal independence
High self-esteem				Low self-esteem
Dynamic fast-moving atmosphere				Staid, slow-moving atmosphere
High 'customer' service focus				Low 'customer' service focus
High intra-organisational competition				Low organisational competition
Very open to change				Very resistant to change

A = acquirer

B = acquired

Culture implications at the individual level

In the amount of restraint placed upon individuals, there is a continuum of cultural types. These are represented in Figure 4.18.

Fig. 4.18 Amount of restraint upon individuals and culture type

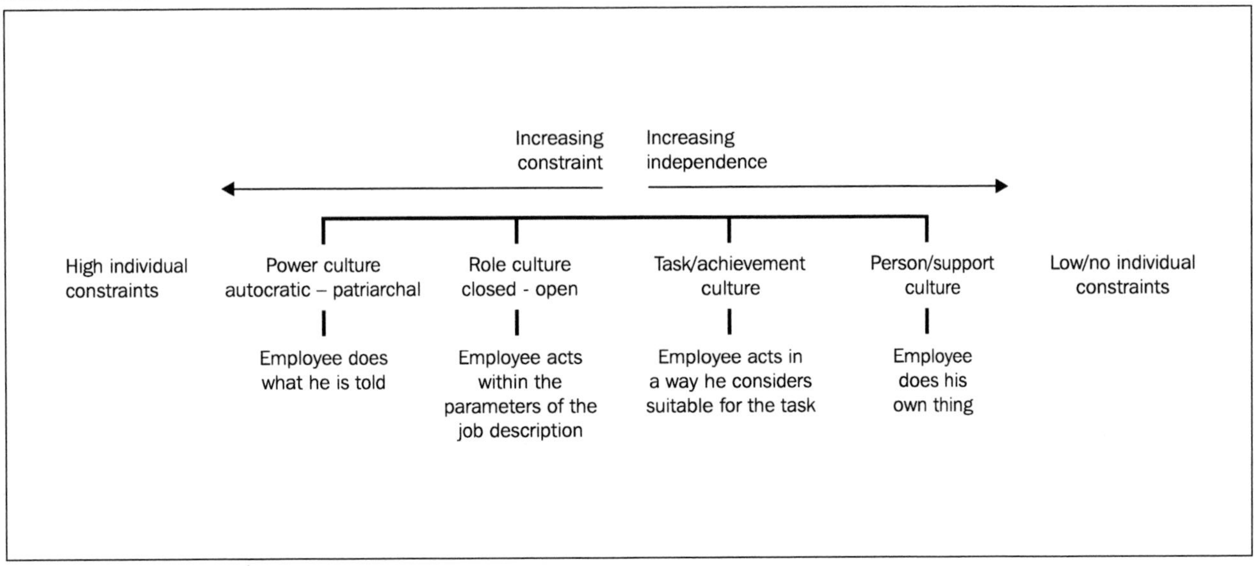

Source: Cartwright and Cooper (1992: 75). Reproduced by kind permission of Butterworth Heinemann from *Mergers and Acquisitions – The Human Factor*

By plotting the relative position of both companies on the continuum, one can assess the degree of similarity/dissimilarity between the two. Cultural similarity in itself is not a prerequisite of successful integration. The key issue is the distance and direction in which the acquired company has to move. In particular, the extent to which the culture of the acquired organisation is supposed to adapt, results in more or fewer constraints being imposed upon individual employees. This will have an immediate effect upon employees' attitudes.

There are mitigating factors in the willingness of employees to abandon their old culture and the extent to which the new culture is attractive. Figure 4.19 predicts a set of outcomes.

Fig. 4.19 Types of organisational and individual acculturation, with potential outcomes

		Willingness of employees to abandon their old culture	
		Very willing	Not at all willing
Perception of 'attractiveness' of the other culture	Very attractive	**Assimilation** Potentially smooth transition	**Integration** Culture collision v. Satisfactory integration/fusion
	Not at all attractive	**Deculturation** Alienation	**Separation** Culture collision. Satisfactory tolerance of multiculturalism

Source: Cartwright and Cooper, 1992: 79). Adapted from Nahavandi and Malekzadeh (1988) *Academy of Management Review*, 13, No. 1. By kind permission of Butterworth Heinemann Publishers from *Mergers and Acquisitions – The Human Factor*

Force field analysis

When comparisons between companies have been carried out, through use of the cultural web or cultural profiling, to identify similarities and differences, the extent of change will be largely determined by the degree of integration which is intended. If there is a need to make changes to the acquired company's culture, or indeed that of the parent, it will be useful to carry out a force field analysis to identify the forces which will help promote or retard change. From Figure 4.20 overleaf, issues such as good communications and flexible structures can help to aid cultural change. Teams can play a very useful role in helping to integrate different cultures by physically involving members from both companies in achieving a common goal (see later).

Fig. 4.20 Force field analysis

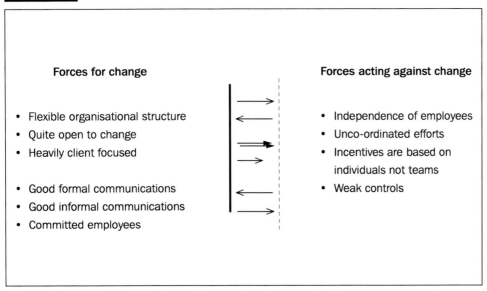

Source: Adapted from Johnson and Scholes (1999: 508). Reproduced by kind permission of the authors, from *Exploring Corporate Strategy*, 5th Edition, Pearson Education Ltd., Prentice Hall Europe

The beginnings of a change programme

Identifying cultural similarities and differences is just the beginning of a change programme. Altering cultures can, and very often does, take years. In some cases the transformation is never complete. However, in these initial stages of taking charge, it is critical for:

■ a shared need to be created

■ employees to buy into the new vision

■ employees to be mobilised into make change happen.

It is only by gaining employees' commitment that they will be willing to invest very considerable amounts of time, energy and patience in what can be a difficult process and one which they may perceive to be risky.

Beyond this stage, companies can begin to embark on full business transformations, if this is the intended integration style. Some effective models for business transformation are the Balanced Scorecard (Kaplan and Norton, 1992), and its many variants, the 4 Rs of Transformation (Gouillart and Kelly, 1995), Five Factors for Change (Pettigrew and Whipp, 1991).

It is very likely that in the early days there will be something of a performance down-turn as old ways are discarded and new ways are not yet fully learnt. This can be demoralising and requires careful and supportive handling. However, clear direction and supporting actions will bring their rewards as small successes and increasing confidence build momentum for greater achievements.

The use of integration teams

There appears to be almost universal recommendation of the use of teams in post-acquisition integration. However, there is no generally accepted terminology to describe teams. This has resulted in a range of labels: interface teams; task forces; transition teams; integration teams; project teams. The extent and nature of roles for teams also vary widely depending upon the style of integration intended. Where teams are used, at one extreme there may be just a small, high-level interface team, which liaises between the two organisations, and a task force that oversees minor change in the acquired company. At the other extreme, there may be several hundred teams involving thousands of people. For instance, in the SmithKline Beecham merger, there were in excess of 250 task forces involving over 2000 people world-wide (Bauman, Jackson, Lawrence, 1997).

This section will look primarily at the second tier of teams, below the interface management team, which was discussed earlier. Here we shall examine:

- the value of teams
- the use of teams
- setting up teams
- team work process
- team longevity
- team size
- team resources.

The relationship between the use of these teams and different post-acquisition integration styles is highlighted in the next chapter.

The value of teams

Teams can play an invaluable role in post-acquisition management. They are excellent for:

- interfacing between companies
- handling complexity
- facilitating smooth integration
- driving change down into an organisation.

Coopers and Lybrand's survey (1996) shows that transition teams give members a stake in the integration and communicate commitment. A recent study by London Consulting Ltd (1998) also suggests that using teams may be associated with higher rates of success in more complex post-acquisition integrations. This may be linked to their finding that, in complex integrations, teams were associated with fewer phases of post-acquisition change, and the integration process was completed more rapidly, than where teams had not been used. This finding seems to be counter to the often cited view that teams are slow. It would seem that they may build a better awareness of the real extent of the complexity in the integration task and then are able to provide more effective solutions.

The use of teams

There are no studies to date which have explicitly matched type of team to different post-acquisition integration challenges. However, the study by London Consulting Ltd (1998) suggests that there are close links between more sophisticated team structures and a combination of the size and complexity (in structural and organisational terms) of the companies, the degree of difference between the companies and the extent to which they are to be integrated. This supports the evidence above that the main value of teams is perceived to be in the handling of complex issues.

Setting up teams

Setting up teams as soon as possible is in line with being prepared upon taking charge to hit the ground running. Professional acquirers set up integration teams in advance and try to negotiate pre-closing access. In complex integrations, it is more than likely that the acquirer will wish to use substantial numbers of acquired employees and this will probably have to be arranged shortly after closing. These formalised joint integration teams may well spawn further subsidiary teams, sometimes called 'jiglets', to investigate unexpected or particularly problematic issues. Whilst teams might be organised in a variety of ways, it would seem that the most common format is a hierarchical one (see Figure 4.21).

Fig. 4.21 Idealised diagram of a set of integration teams

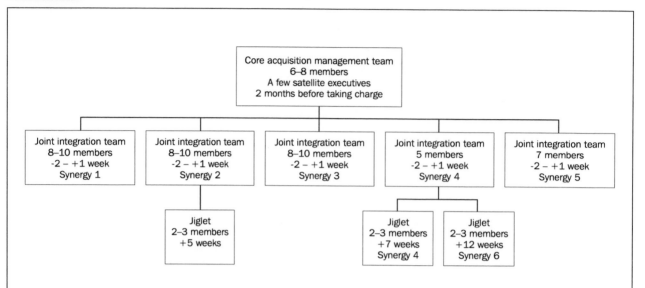

Note: Dates refer to set-up time relative to completion date

Core acquisition management team: this team's overall role is to co-ordinate the post-acquisition integration process. Its membership will consist of the key managers who will lead the integration and will either report to the main board and/or will include main board members.

Secondary layer of joint integration teams: these may have a number of orientations, depending upon how the benefits from the integration are perceived. For this reason, they may be based on functional lines, process issues, a combination of the two, or be focused upon specific synergy realisations and business opportunities. The degree of similarity between business structures and the degree of integration intended will influence this decision.

Tertiary layer of joint integration teams: these jiglets tend to arise as further potential integration benefits are uncovered, or unanticipated difficulties surface. In many circumstances, they arise from the wish of employees to investigate an issue rather than from senior managers identifying and setting up a task. As a result, jiglets pop up in different places at different times throughout the process. They also dissolve themselves when the task is done.

Team work process

It is important that teams have a defined purpose which is broken down into objectives and key issues. This can be set up as a series of charters. Teams can then follow a process involving data gathering and comparisons to enable recommendations to be passed to the core acquisition management team for approval. The importance of the joint data gathering is that it enables executives from both sides to begin to appreciate the significant differences in working practices and core assumptions.

Fig. 4.22 Team work process

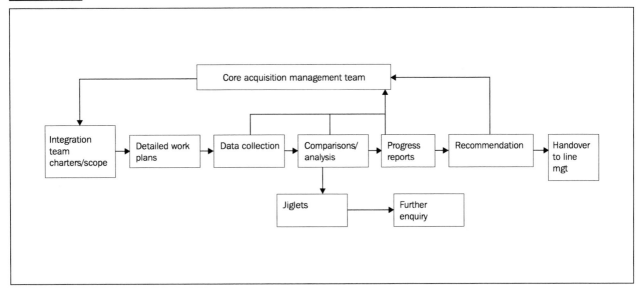

Team longevity

The longevity of the teams will reflect the nature of the tasks they are involved in. Where a task is well-defined, with a concrete set of deliverables, the team may be short lived. However, if the task is ill-defined, owing to the nature of the problem, and the outcomes uncertain, the team may exist for quite some time, although its progress should be well monitored. However, in the words of one CEO, *'They tend to die a natural death'* as they satisfy their objectives. The differences in the type of task set for teams will reflect the integration style.

Team size

The optimal numbers for a team to operate effectively are often cited as between five and six executives. London Consulting (1998) found that half of the top integration teams they surveyed were of this size, with a further 25 per cent having up to ten members. Half of the teams met at least two to three times a week and a further 25 per cent weekly. Most of the members of the team were involved on a part-time basis.

Secondary teams (joint integration teams) tended to vary more widely in size, but seemed to be generally larger than the top integration team. In nearly all cases, the members were part-time, and they held meetings at least once a week. The team tended to last around 6 months, although in some cases the team survived well into the second year. Tertiary teams (jiglets) were smaller than the secondary teams.

Team resources

An important component of effective team work is an appropriate level of independence for the task. Where the task is open and complex, teams will require significant autonomy to achieve results. Linked to this is the need for a running budget and in some cases an equipment budget.

Employees participating in the teams did not seem to require significant rewards for their efforts, although in some instances these were given. It would seem that being involved and having the opportunity to broaden their experience was sufficient reward in itself.

A word of caution

Tokenism is never to be recommended. In a few isolated instances, merging companies have used teams in a rather cynical way to give employees the illusion that they are helping with the integration. Whilst this may help morale and dampen the effects of the rumour mill in the early stages of the post-merger phase, employees rapidly realise the 'sham' when all their hard work, often fitted in around their jobs, is ignored. This severely erodes trust in top management and dampens enthusiasm and commitment to the new organisation. New barriers to integration have been created.

Teams can be a powerful force for effective, lasting change. In the words of a group chief accountant, *'teams tend to be more efficient than individuals in providing recommendations and executing them'*. They ease the transition process and *'act as facilitators rather than victims of change'*.

CHAPTER 4: SUMMARY

- Appoint a senior executive with specific responsibility, resources and time for overseeing the entire acquisition process.
- Hit the ground running via good pre-acquisition planning for the post-acquisition phase.
- Use the window of opportunity just before closing to deepen links and set up joint integration teams.
- Protect your investment by establishing interface management.
- Take charge clearly, positively and rapidly.
- Stabilise the acquisition and manage employee expectations through clear leadership, vision, commitment and excellent communications.
- Find out what you have bought, rather than assume you know.

- Build cultural awareness and establish the foundations for change.
- Recognise the multiple virtues of teams.

Notes

1   An issue close to many companies' hearts is the transfer of knowledge between companies. This is very often assessed at face value, without appreciating that it is context bound. The knowledge may well have different meaning in a different context.

2   Float times are the amount of leeway between the earliest and latest start times.

3   Taking charge can mean different things to different executives. For some, it is a process that lasts years and includes complete business, organisational and cultural transformation. We believe there is a value in distinguishing between immediate and reasonably standard actions, and longer-term, more varied adjustments.

4   In many cases the acquisition will also cause the world to change for the acquiring company, although it may not have recognised this at the time of the deal. New possibilities and *constraints* are the result of marriage.

5   Emphasis is the author's.

6   Emphasis is the author's.

7   This scale runs from static media (general to personal) to interactive media (general to personal).

8   It is important to note that the converse is *not implied*, namely that if downsizing is intended, then employee uncertainty is acceptable. This can only damage the attitude and morale of those remaining.

9   The extent of communications possible will be determined primarily by whether the deal is private or public, hostile or friendly.

10   There was variation between companies depending upon environmental and corporate complexity. For instance, a simple structure with stable conditions would have just financial controls. More complexity and instability would lead in turn to actual costing, responsibility accounting, inflation accounting, flexible budgets, operational budgets, long-range, contingency and strategic plans.

5

What to change in different acquisition styles?

PRIORITISING CHANGES

Once stabilisation actions have been taken, which items should be changed first? Many acquirers have a number of rules of thumb for prioritising actions which we shall review below. However, acquirers should be aware of the post-acquisition tension between:

the urge or perceived need for quick wins

versus

harder critical changes for realising the acquisition's purpose

Caution

The rules of thumb are standard methods, which can be damaging if applied uncritically. In particular, there is a tendency for the well intentioned pursuit of value drivers to be translated within the organisations into the pursuit of narrow financial targets. In many cases, acquirers need to guard against this if the purpose of the acquisition is not to be overridden.

Generally, prioritising changes upon acquisition assumes that all the assumptions made about the acquired company are correct. This is unlikely. Acquirers need a mechanism for assessing their assumptions in the early stages of the integration.

Finally, the attraction of rules of thumb is that they reduce complexity to easily understood and communicable forms. However, this simplification often leads to an understatement of linkages between various changes. Understating inter-connectedness can result in changes having an unexpected and extended impact.

Pareto rule

The Pareto rule has a value in the post-acquisition phase. The window of opportunity for carrying out changes relating to the acquisition will tend to deteriorate over time as *'newness is a wasting asset'*. However, the choice of synergies to aim for needs to be made. To be efficient and realistically achievable, consultants advise acquirers to focus upon the 20 per cent of synergies that will generate 80 per cent of the expected return. However, these aims are often coloured by the ease or difficulty of making such changes work successfully.

Impact versus speed

Ideally acquirers prefer to carry out changes which have a high impact on performance outcome and can be quickly put in place with minimum disruption. Such 'quick wins' can help build confidence within the organisation and, importantly, send strong signals to investors about the apparent effectiveness of the integration. These early successes can also help to provide momentum for longer-term and more difficult changes. Figure 5.1 shows an impact versus speed matrix.

Fig. 5.1 Impact versus speed matrix

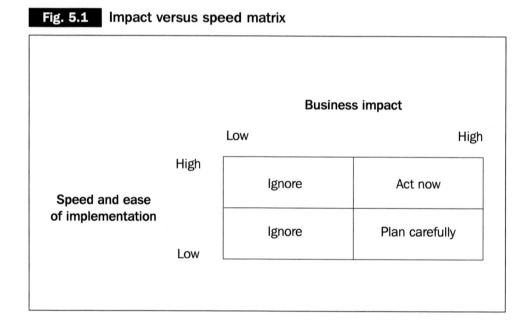

Risk priority matrix

Implementing major changes can be very risky. For this reason it is useful also to assess risk formally. The main issues are:

- quantifying the cost of the risk;
- assessing the likelihood of the risk occurring;
- time scale within which risk may occur.

Figure 5.2 shows the mitigating effect of risk upon our impact versus speed matrix.

Fig. 5.2 Risk priority matrix

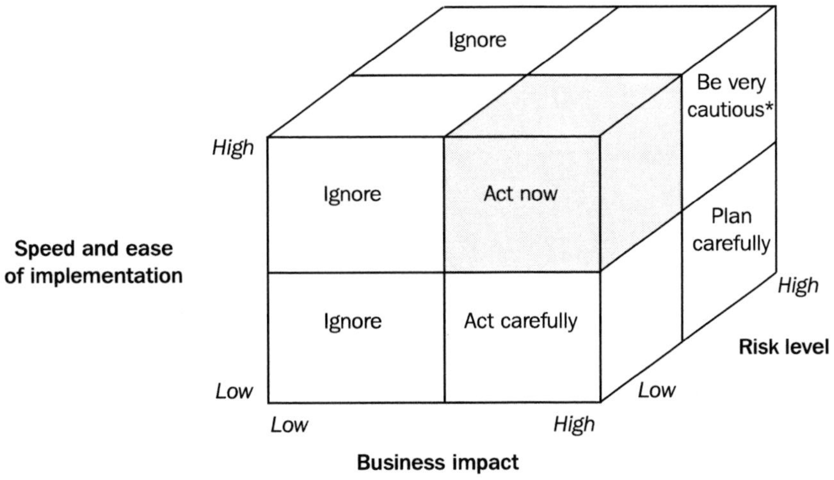

* Ensure there is a defined solution

Summary

These broad rules of thumb are just that and should not be applied uncritically. In particular, such techniques should not override the strategic purpose of the acquisition. In the next section we point out some of the advantages and disadvantages of quick wins and recommend that they play a subservient role to changes which reflect specific acquisition styles.

Quick wins

Pressure to focus upon quick wins comes from a perceived need felt by top management to signal to analysts and investors that they were right to back the change in control and that the group is on course to recover acquisition premiums.[1] Quick wins may also be perceived as a useful signal to employees that there will be change and change for the better. In this sense, it helps to remove uncertainty and provide tangible evidence that the acquirer is taking charge. There might also be an element of top management gaining confidence from such actions.

The downside of quick wins is that they may be identified by an acquirer who assumes too much about the way in which the acquired business operates. Apparent inefficiencies may conceal value. In particular, focusing upon specific areas to cut frequently results in underestimating the interconnections between activities and resources and so the widespread implications of such cuts. A popular quick win is to reduce the workforce. This is normally achieved by a very narrow definition of what employees do. Many acquirers subsequently discover that important tacit knowledge, about how the company operates effectively, has been lost. For this reason, we often hear of the very same employees being re-hired later, or brought back as consultants on open-ended arrangements and at inflated salaries!

There is also the possibility that the hunt for quick wins is perceived by employees as 'the' strategic change programme rather than an exercise to build confidence on several levels so that the main changes can be tackled with greater confidence. If considerable time is spent achieving quick wins and then ironing out problems that result from these actions, the 'will' to engage in further more complex change will have been substantially eroded.

Quick wins then may result in short-term uplifts in performance, which top management can use to assuage the concerns of investors and analysts. However, such quick wins can result in medium-term costs:

- unanticipated linkages causing more widespread disruption than anticipated;
- loss of tacit knowledge. Eroding functionality and the capability base;
- distracting attention from the main strategic areas of change.

Critical change to realise the acquisition's purpose

It is vital not to lose sight of the purpose of the acquisition. However, it is undeniable that post-acquisition, especially where substantial acquisition premiums have been paid, top management feel under considerable pressure to begin to recoup the balance. The profound problem with this is that the acquirer can very quickly become locked into a narrow financial logic of cutting costs to remove this pressure. Whilst cutting costs can be achieved rapidly and with degrees of certainty, this can significantly damage the strategic logic of the acquisition.

It requires top management of real calibre to be able to occupy the difficult space between the external pressures of investors clamouring for evidence of financial improvements and the internal pressures of having to take charge, show direction and reduce uncertainties, whilst embarking upon difficult, time-consuming and often quite uncertain change for medium-term strategic advantage.

Assuming then that the acquired company turns out to be entirely as expected (and this is quite an assumption!), the acquirer needs to be quite clear about the main drivers of change necessary to achieve the strategic purpose. We should advise against being too quick to ascribe purely financial outcomes to these drivers, as many strategic aims are not easily reducible to a financial uplift. When these drivers are clear, we recommend using these as the basis for a change programme rather than being seduced by quick wins.

WHO SHOULD MANAGE THE ACQUIRED COMPANY?

There is no doubt that there is considerable turnover in the top management of acquired companies after acquisition. In his study of 200 acquisitions by Fortune 500 members, Hayes (1979) recorded that only 42 per cent of top managers remained with their company five years after acquisition. More recent studies have found that 67 per cent of all acquired senior executives had left within four years in major acquisitions in the US (Hambrick and Cannella, 1993) and 57 per cent of acquired chief executives were no longer in their positions two years after the deal in the 100 largest acquisitions in the UK, 1990–4 (Angwin, 1996a).[2]

Whilst there is significantly higher turnover amongst the top management of acquired companies than non-acquired companies, there is less agreement on whether top management should be changed. For instance, McCann and Gilkey (1988) in their study of Allied-Signal Corporation, supplemented with detail on eight other acquisitions, argue that *'Comprehensive changes in top management are often crucial for acquisition success'*. On the other hand, Anslinger and Copeland's (1996: 130) study, of 829 acquisitions made by 21 successful acquirers, shows that pre-acquisition managers were kept in nearly 85 per cent of cases.

Clearly there is disagreement over whether top management should stay or go.

The case for changing acquired top management

In line with the 'conquering hero syndrome', there is a prevalent view that acquiring top managers are superior to the acquired top managers and therefore that the former can manage the businesses of the latter for greater value. This view might be best seen in hostile take-overs where there are clear differences over the way in which the acquired business should be managed. Unsurprisingly, 90 per cent of directors resign after hostile bids (Franks and Mayer, 1996) as against 50 per cent in accepted bids. However, Franks and Mayer (1996) conclude that, rather than the acquired top managers necessarily being poor performers prior to acquisition, the high levels of boardroom change reflect disagreements over asset redeployment after the acquisition. A good illustration of this might be Granada's bid for Trust House Forte, where the latter was showing promising changes prior to take-over but had radically different views from the aggressor over the future deployment of assets.

Changing the acquired top management then is linked to intentions to carry out substantial changes to the acquired business. It recognises incumbent top management as a potential impediment to change as they are seen to be synonymous with their company's past strategy and way of operating. Although incumbent top management may indeed have managed their businesses well, they are likely to be scape-goated for the loss of their company's independence and so removed. The appointment of a new chief executive is a signal to stakeholders that he will be a potent force for change.

Using new chief executives, who are drawn from outside of the acquired organisation (Outsiders), is necessary, as Insiders are reluctant to impose radical change. In the words of one Outsider CEO of an acquired manufacturing business, '*As an Outsider you can stand back and see things, often clearer, in a visionary strategic sense*'.

Empirical evidence has shown that Outsiders are associated with higher levels of post-acquisition change as well as more radical change (Angwin, 1998b). They also have the advantage, if drawn from the parent company, of understanding how the parent works and how to communicate with it effectively.

Often Outsiders have a mandate for change; it is the basis upon which they have been brought in and new brooms need to be seen to take charge. There is an expectation of change both from above and below. The Outsider is also not tied to personal allegiances in the acquired company and is less restricted in his ability to take action.

> *Outsiders are not encumbered by the burden of the acquired company's past history. You've got the advantage (over an Insider) of being totally objective and you haven't got personal allegiances which I think is underestimated in business. As a newcomer you don't have that emotional burden. (Outsider in charge of a large acquired services business)*

When the Outsider makes changes, this is often on a much greater scale than the Insider.

> *I think we felt the changes were pretty substantial and it needed a new person, new blood, to implement that. If the management had just stayed the same, although they bought into the changes, I think they would have found it very difficult when push came to shove, to actually do it. (Outsider CEO of a media company)*

The challenge for the Outsider is to get to grips with the acquired company and understand how it functions, whilst at the same time actively taking charge. The tension and uncertainty in the acquired company as well as the need to move the business into unfamiliar waters will more than likely result in a performance downturn.

The stock market recognises the potential upheaval caused by changing CEOs and share prices often react negatively when a chief executive is changed (Beatty and Zajac, 1987). Major problems can occur with the installation of an Outsider in terms of resentment and a deterioration in morale (Ravenscraft and Sherer,

1987). In a study of 96 acquisitions, Cannella and Hambrick (1993) have shown that the departure of senior executives affects company performance negatively, and Krishnan, Miller and Judge's (1997) examination of 147 acquisitions found that turnover in top management teams is negatively related to post-acquisition performance. See Figure 5.3.

Fig. 5.3 Indicative post-acquisition performance in an acquired company experiencing significant change

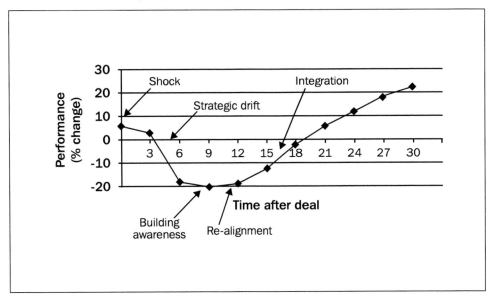

Note: This figure is intended only to describe the performance decline and later resurgence, assuming changes have taken place, rather than prescribe actual values or timing. Estimates range from 6 months (Rankine, 1998) to 18 months to reach the lowest point of performance.

The case for retaining acquired top management

Retaining incumbent management can be seen to smooth the passage of post-acquisition integration. Keeping the Insider is often seen as a vote of confidence in the way in which the acquired company has been run. The acquisition itself therefore is much less of a driver for change. *'They (the acquirer) didn't interfere with the business. They just let me run the company'* (Insider CEO of an acquisition in the manufacturing sector). *'There wasn't that much to change 'cause it (the acquired business) was very successful and even now it's still going along the same track. There was nothing for them to do, so they were quite happy'* (Insider CEO of an acquisition in the distribution sector).

The evidence seems to suggest, therefore, that where incumbents remain, acquisitions will tend to be more successful than where they are replaced. The reasons are that the acquired company is already successful and the parent is unlikely to interfere with its running, post-acquisition. On the other hand, the radical change or anticipated change associated with Outsiders is likely to result in a downturn in performance before the new strategic direction pays off. Maintaining the strategic apex, keeping incumbent management or promoting internally, will, in the short term, be more successful than using Outsiders in the post-acquisition phase.

Insiders/Outsiders and speed of change

Whilst Outsiders make more radical changes to the acquired company, there is evidence that Insiders make changes more rapidly than Outsiders (see Table 5.1). For 94 per cent of all changes surveyed in acquired companies 1990–4, Insiders acted more rapidly than Outsiders[3] (Angwin, 1995b).

Table 5.1 Functional areas in which Insiders act significantly faster than Outsiders

Functional area	% of items where Insiders acted more rapidly than Outsiders
Finance	85.7
Marketing	100.0
Communications	100.0
Human resources	78.6
Operations	100.0
I.T.	100.0

Insiders tend to make changes more rapidly than Outsiders, as they are far more familiar with their companies, whereas Outsiders need time to build a picture. In some cases Outsiders are not informed of their new appointments until a day or so before the acquisition happens! As a result, time is essential to build an understanding of the acquired company. '*We broadly knew what to do but not enough to go in there and do it on day 1*' (Outsider of an acquisition in the drinks manufacturing sector). Where Outsiders have a reasonable knowledge of the acquisition, there is still a need for time to ensure that assumptions are correct.

> *I went into the acquisition with an open mind. (Outsider of an acquisition in the water industry)*

Insiders often made changes that they had been wanting to carry out for a long time but for which they needed an excuse. In one instance a CEO wanted to remove the finance director as he was perceived to be poor. However, as the finance director was a substantial shareholder, he was difficult to remove. This situation altered with a change in control. In the words of another Insider,

> *It helps to be able to pin redundancy decisions upon the acquiring company's personnel department in Head Office. (Insider of an acquisition in the engineering industry)*

There is also an argument that the Insider does not take his eye off the commercial football to the same extent as an Outsider who has to learn about the business. On this basis the Insider may be more responsive to changes in the market. Commenting on changes made to the business during the post-acquisition period,

> *We were making changes because I thought it was appropriate to make changes. It was not the parent telling us. I continually change an organisation, it's never static. (Insider of an acquisition in the engineering industry)*

However, negotiating the acquisition does absorb a great deal of senior management time, so the retained Insider often feels, once the deal is completed, that he has to get back into the saddle.

> *The business had suffered from me being out of involvement (whilst) I tried to sell it. I had to get re-involved. Because I had more time to spend on the business I was able to identify what needed doing next and to drive it forward, which I had not sufficient time to do in the past. (Insider of an acquisition in the engineering industry)*

Finally the Insider already has a working network, both within his business, as informal communications channels, as well as external relationships. This is vital for implementing agendas. The Outsider, however, needs time to construct such a system. Although the next quotation is more about which managers to remove or keep, it points to the in-built delay in action as well as the need to create some sort of interface.

> *We need to spend five months establishing exactly who the right people are. We know broadly the structure that we want, but let's create some interface between the organisations that allows us to start the planning process. (Outsider of an acquisition in the food and drinks industry)*

Insider/Outsider summary

Clearly there are profound differences between Insiders and Outsiders. It is important to note that one is not necessarily better than the other in the post-acquisition period, but that they do different things. For instance, where there is an intention to carry out substantial change to the acquired company which will re-configure its nature, then the Outsider may well be the most appropriate manager. Where the intention is generally to leave the acquired company alone and to learn from it, then retaining the Insider makes more sense. In other words, there are 'horses for courses'. The appropriateness of Insider and Outsider will be shown in the next section, which examines the milestones in different acquisition types.

MILESTONES IN EACH ACQUISITION STYLE

The pattern of change for each acquisition type is quite different in terms of the volume of changes that occur, as well as the speed. Figure 5.4 shows when changes were initiated[4] for the four post-acquisition styles, based upon acquisitions in the UK, 1990–4.

Fig. 5.4 Timing and volume of change by acquisition type

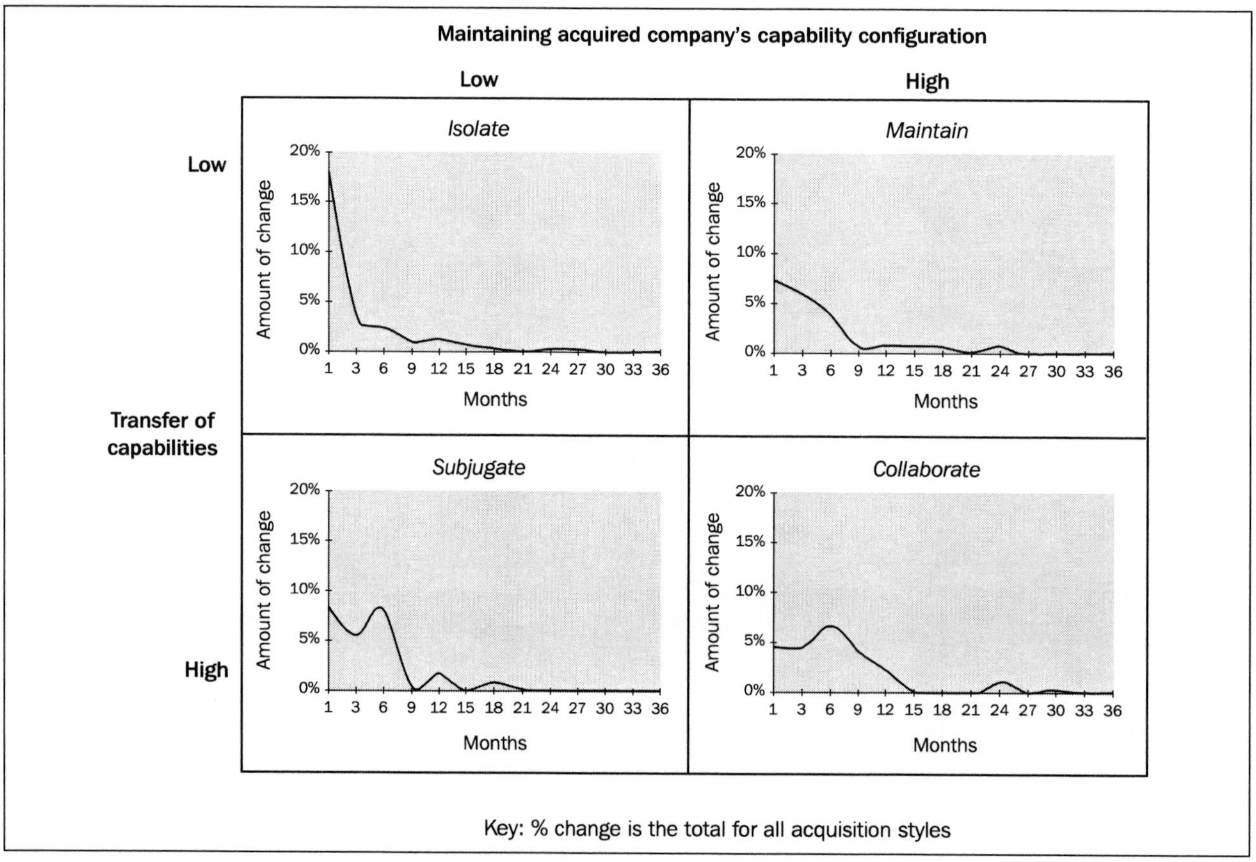

Source: Angwin (1998)

Each acquisition style has a different time frame for when most change takes place and for how long initiation of changes continues to take place. From Figure 5.4 we can see that acquired companies that lose the original configuration of their acquired capabilities see rapid and substantial change. Those companies which retain the original configuration of their capabilities see much less intense change starts, which then continue over a longer period.

Each of the following sections shows key actions for each of the post-acquisition styles.

ISOLATION ACQUISITIONS

Acquired companies which are put into isolation are frequently characterised by financial weakness and are in different but related businesses to the parent company. In many cases the acquirer has seen an opportunity to carry out a turnaround, but to avoid contaminating the rest of the parent group, the acquired company is kept in isolation. In order to achieve the turnaround, isolation acquisitions require rapid and sweeping change with an overriding aim of achieving financial soundness.

Timing of changes in isolation acquisitions

Fig. 5.5 Isolation acquisition – when changes start

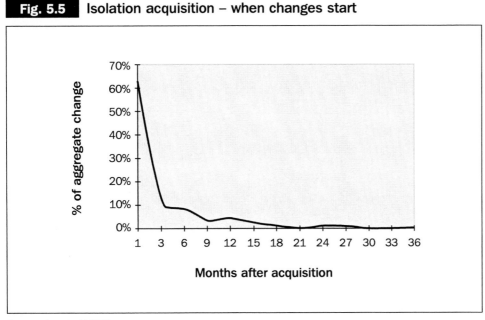

Source: Angwin (1998)

Figure 5.5 shows the rapidity with which change is started in isolation acquisitions. 62 per cent of change in these acquisitions is initiated in the first month.

Preventing further deterioration is critical. An Insider at an industrial land usage firm describes this as:

> *Stabilising the workforce, stopping capital expenditure, stopping financial misuse, putting immediate controls on the finances and putting in place the parent required financial systems.*

Speed of action is clearly vital to reverse poor financial health and can be across the board. In the words of an Insider at an acquired financial services company,

> *Have a clear idea and do it. You'll get lots wrong, but that doesn't actually matter. People want clarity.*

Changes made in isolation acquisitions

Review acquired top management

The incumbent managing executive almost always remains with this acquisition type, as they can achieve things quickly. This reflects the need for a rapid reverse in the declining fortunes of the business. In the words of an Insider at an electronics company,

> *I had been thinking about making changes for months and I had got a blueprint already in place and I just pressed the button.*

The new parent also recognises that the acquired business is different to their own. However, the world has changed for the incumbent managing executive who is spurred on by the new parent to achieve results. The change is particularly noticeable in his strategic horizon which tends to collapse. The Insider now manages for short-term performance targets rather than for any medium- or long-term strategic goals.

Although the incumbent managing executive often remains, there are major changes in the management team. Around 80 per cent of isolation acquisitions experience re-assignments of senior executives and 90 per cent see redundancies at this level. Amongst the redundancies, the finance director in particular, but also marketing and sales directors, are often casualties. The former often leaves as the business is in a poor financial condition, and the latter leaves as attempts to improve performance in the market are critical for success.

Improve financial controls

The main driver in isolation acquisitions is to cut back to the core business, to reduce costs and return the business to a more healthy footing. Direct financial controls are given the utmost priority and budgets are very closely controlled and monitored. In the words of one acquiring parent company CEO,

> *I wouldn't let any of the controls slip. I wouldn't tolerate any departure. We don't let that get away.*

The focus is short-term improvements in results at all costs.

Many acquired company managing executives complain about the stringency and unyielding nature of parental controls, which seem to have little bearing upon their business. In the words of an Insider CEO of an acquired engineering consultancy,

> *We were constrained by the parent company, not free to make decisions in the best interests of our business. The parent company imposed rigid expenditure controls.*

The case study that follows (Case study 5.1) shows the constraints and severity of these new controls with the Insider managing executive being forced to make severe changes in order to meet budget although with damaging consequences in the medium term.

90 per cent of isolation acquisitions impose a tight control on overheads and production costs. As the managing director of an acquired industrial services company said,

> *The rationale for the changes was of course the company was making losses basically because the overheads and the management overheads were too big.*

Improved quality and service

About 50 per cent of isolation acquisitions reduce delivery days and introduce after sales service. There is also effort applied to improving the product design. Clearly there is some emphasis upon improving quality and service, although attention appears to be on the items which are easier and quicker to change.

Improved marketing

Isolation acquisitions see considerable attempts to improve distribution as this can lead to rapid improvements in results. Despite efforts to improve delivery and the customer interface, there is, curiously, less emphasis on improving marketing information to the parent board. This may be explained by the fact that the Insider is trying to defend the marketing effort from the financial rigours imposed by the parent company. Generally improving marketing assumes a rather muted role in isolation acquisitions. In the words of the Insider of a manufacturing business,

> *The parent company imposed rigid expenditure controls, staffing policies and marketing initiatives were denied.*

A good example of the tensions between meeting financial targets and the acquired CEO's perception of the strategic importance of marketing and development is illustrated by the Insider managing an acquisition in the electronics manufacturing sector. He found the most difficult changes were reductions in development and marketing,

> *because it was hitting the future of the company. I found that very hard to explain to people because I'd always preached sales are critical to pay our salaries but the real future in the company is what we are ploughing back in from cashflow to product and market development – and here I was just putting a great line through my own strategy. The instruction from the parent company was get back to budget.*

Intensive efforts to reduce costs

89 per cent of isolation acquisitions see cuts in head office staff. This is part of the rationalisation process, justified on the basis of the duplication of function or sub-optimal performance, and the removal of barriers to change. The managing director of an acquired industrial services company said,

> *The plan was to close down the head office, which was very expensive and opulent. That was a fairly major task but not very difficult to do. The company was in fact making losses – it had had a few cutbacks and they basically got rid of the lower paid staff and kept a lot of managers – it was very top heavy. So we did have to remove a lot of top management.*

Over half of isolation acquisitions see efforts to reduce production costs through better control of production, stock and capacity utilisation.

The reporting systems are sacrosanct. They've all been brought in. We're also bringing in unprecedented performance monitoring systems. Every single truck, every single system, every single type of container through the accounting procedures can be broken out, can be assessed in their entirety, on their own. You can pull out any type, any feature of our business to see where it is losing money. Everything has to be performance monitored. Everything is very, very accountable. There is accountability for everything and everybody. We didn't have that before. (MD of an acquired industrial land usage)

Restructuring is a common factor in isolation acquisitions with a view to improving the efficiency of the core operation. The managing director of an acquired industrial services company remarked that,

We removed three quarters of the directors as they were in areas where there were too many divisions and not enough activity. So we quickly restructured into sales and purchasing rather than product divisions.

The main aim of this type of restructuring is to achieve greater efficiencies. This may include improving plant, although capital investment tends to be rare. There is, however, some investment in better training and wage incentives to improve productivity. The managing director of an acquired industrial services company remarked that,

This is something I set up. They have bonuses related to the profit of the division which has a monthly charge on it, which is a percentage of the net assets used in the division. It's made everyone very conscious of the working capital which is used in the business.

Reduction in debt

The vast majority of isolation acquisitions sell off subsidiaries to reduce debt and return the company to a sound financial footing. The managing director at an acquired industrial services company said,

There was a division which was selling machines which no-one really felt was going to fit in very well with the industrial machinery business and we didn't think it was going to work out so we closed that down.

The pressure to reduce debts and restore profitability was succinctly illustrated by the comments of a managing director of a recently acquired electronic component company. In response to the new parent's demands, his attitude was,

> *Cut back, cut back, cut back – but if that's what they want, profit, I'll give them profit, or reduce losses.*

Problems with isolation acquisitions

Following the burst of immediate change used to effect a turnaround, acquired top executives have commented on a loss of strategic direction and momentum. There is often a complete lack of strategic input from the parent company, which leaves the acquired companies in a vacuum. In addition, businesses within the parent group are often compartmentalised,[5] impairing inter-group dialogue and activity. Whilst synergies may have been the reason behind the acquisitions, the mechanisms to enable these to be realised are often just not there.

This post-acquisition lull is illustrated in Figure 5.5, which shows a marked reduction in change towards the third month, a plateau at six months and then a further decline towards the end of the year. Thereafter there is only minor activity.

Lulls following post-acquisition turnarounds occur either because the parent lacks appropriate expertise other than in financial management or because its competence is too different to be applied. In either case there is a generally accepted belief by acquired top management that the parent does not understand the acquired business.

At the acquired company, this post-turnaround lull has deleterious effects. In the words of the managing director of an acquired electronics company, '*We were left in a complete vacuum. All we did was carry on*'. Running weak businesses, subject to severe cuts, erodes the acquired managing executive's voice at group level. They clearly do not feel valued and greatly resent the attendant lack of influence. Their sacrifice of long-term strategy for short-term gain leads to considerable frustration for them, as they feel that their role has been downgraded to managing for short-term results. In general they feel futile and depressed. In one instance known to the author, a former owner manager committed suicide.

Case study 5.1

An isolation acquisition

This case and the succeeding cases have been selected because of the way in which they characterise the nature of specific acquisition styles. Their virtue is the 'realness' of actual situations. However, it should be noted that this approach will emphasise details which may play a less important role in other cases of the same acquisition type. Nevertheless real events make for compelling reading and this is preferred to the more balanced but contrived view of the synthetic case. Readers then should bear in mind that specific details in our cases may not be represented with such force in other circumstances, although the general picture is representative.

Circuit Board PLC acquisition of Transistor PLC

Transistor PLC, a manufacturer of electronics and employing several hundred people, had recently moved into making losses. It was acquired in a friendly take-over by Circuit Board PLC on the grounds that the latter's subsidiary had clear complementary interests.

Post-acquisition, Stanton, CEO of Transistor, said, 'The chap with whom I had been negotiating handed me the Circuit Board PLC procedures, manuals and piles of forms and I said, "Well thank you very much, I was expecting something like this. When can we actually have a meeting to discuss strategy?" He said, "We've got a board meeting coming up in four weeks' time, we'll discuss it then". We never did! I had just one meeting with Circuit Board PLC in the month post-acquisition.

'There was no discussion of strategy which should cover marketing, production, personnel, financial, I mean the whole gambit. They never discussed with me or my other co-directors what we wanted out of the deal and what we were prepared to put in post-acquisition. Nobody came to me and said, "You've built this thing up over the last 20 years, what do you want out of it?" There was no attempt to motivate the staff. It was just "Carry on". People came to me and said, "What now?", "What are they going to do; how can they help us?" and I said, "I have no idea – I'm sure it will all become clear" – but it never did.

'Their financial reporting structure was very good. It was introduced on day one. They required daily cash orders, sales, a report daily and a weekly summary report on P&L. I believe they received far too much information. What was missing was any reaction to those. The only reaction we got was "Group cash is tight, delay paying creditors for another two weeks".'

The first serious discussion was three months post-acquisition at the September board meeting. Transistor was not making budget and the divisional director asked what Stanton was going to do about it. 'I said "I ought to sack half the staff and restructure". He said, "Good idea. Why didn't you do it before?" and I said, "I don't want to get rid of any assets, until I know what you want to do with them". He said, "What we need is to get back on budget!" I said, "The cost of sacking in money terms is X but more importantly in terms of achieving our strategy it's XYZ and means putting back our strategy quite severely." What he said is, "I want profit!"

'When I had the green light to do my pruning exercise I took out the group finance director and group functions as there is no group and fired the co-founder of Transistor, which was a horrible thing to do. I put myself in charge and got rid of half the staff.' Sales and marketing were cut – 'I don't think there was any department that was not touched. I radically cut down the development programme in order to reduce development expenditure by 25 per cent, to make people understand that Circuit Board PLC was after profit short term rather than growth long term. We cut customer and country specific applications. We are paying for it now in that we have lost our market share which has quartered. I downgraded directors' cars, reduced salaries and cut perks. We all took a knock. In my first year I turned Transistor around.'

Other than financial expertise, parent headquarters supplied little else. 'There were things that I was expecting them to encourage such as MRP or quality control systems but none was forthcoming. The main emphasis was on financial controls. Their technology skills were poor and marketers don't exist in Circuit Board PLC.' Nevertheless the corporate style and logo were changed.

Liaisons with other managing directors in the group were not encouraged. 'I said to the divisional managing director, "You've got a very modern factory making electronic equipment, why don't I see if they will do our production for us?" And he said, "Well you know, just carry on as you are, you've got your budgets, there is nothing in the plan for that."'

When Stanton took the initiative to try to realise synergies, he met considerable resistance. 'I phoned up one subsidiary (with synergistic possibilities) to say, "I think we ought to get together. You and I know each other fairly well; I know what you're doing and you know what I'm doing but only on a fairly superficial level. Why don't we get together to see how we can make 2+2 = 5." He said, "That's not my brief. My brief is to continue with the plan and budget I've got and stuff you."'

Post-acquisition, 'We were left in a complete vacuum. All we did was carry on. I had a futile role of managing director. I was exceedingly frustrated and mystified that I never had a discussion with any board member of Circuit Board PLC about the future of the company. Most surprisingly to me was no discussion as to the potential synergy between Transistor and the subsidiary company.'

After pushing for synergy in the division, Stanton was promoted to deputy chairman of the division but in the process lost direct authority to make changes. Whilst he could recommend changes to the managing directors, they were profit responsible for their operations and so no synergy happened.

Isolation acquisition summary

Whilst many acquirers expect their isolation acquisitions to result in operating synergies being realised, success for isolation acquisitions is often more narrow in terms of buying cheaply a badly performing company which the parent is able to turnaround through the imposition of tough controls. For this reason, isolation acquisitions are characterised by intense, focused change, almost 'kill or cure' in nature. The general intention is to improve greatly what is already being done, rather than trying to do things differently. This conservatism reflects the necessity for short time scales, a lack of resources in the acquired company, and an unwillingness of the parent to commit many resources. The mentality is 'retrenchment' rather than 'build'.

The short-term necessity of turnaround also has a dark side in that the broader strategic view beyond the turnaround is often lost or becomes inappropriate. The acquired top management lose much of their voice due to their company's performance and the parent's agendas move on. For this reason, following turnaround, the acquired company has a strong sense of operating in a void.

The ultimate fate of such acquisitions is that they are either sold off many years later, as not fitting the group, or new top management in the parent re-visit the original logic of the deal and insist upon synergies being realised, again, many years after acquisition.

Isolation acquisitions: Main themes

- Retain the managing executive.
- High levels of change to achieve turnaround in financial health:
  meet budget
  change senior management
  restructure divisions
  rationalise assets
  cut expenditure – in marketing, R&D.
- Change in acquired top management perspective from medium to short term.
- Beyond the turnaround a post-acquisition lull:
  no strategic direction
  just carry on and meet budget
  no one driving synergies.

	Acquisition's strategic independence	
	Low	High
Low Capability interaction	Isolate	Maintain
High	Subjugate	Collaborate

MAINTENANCE ACQUISITIONS

Most maintenance acquisitions represent an expansion into new business areas as a platform for further expansion and/or to acquire new capability bases. In many cases parent companies believe they can realise the synergies of closely linked, related diversification, but these often turn out to be far more elusive than expected.

As this type of acquisition represents moving into less familiar business territory, acquirers are generally more cautious about their targets and so look for acquisitions with the hygiene factors of strong financial performance, very significant market presence and quality management.

As a rule, targets are purchased on the grounds of their strengths and so post-acquisition management is characterised by the wish not to disturb the way they are run. In particular, the core capability remains intact and, indeed, is defended by incumbent management against change by the parent. The emphasis is very much to keep things as they are, as they work. The level of change in maintenance acquisitions is therefore low.

Timing of changes in maintenance acquisitions

Fig. 5.6   Maintenance acquisition – when changes start

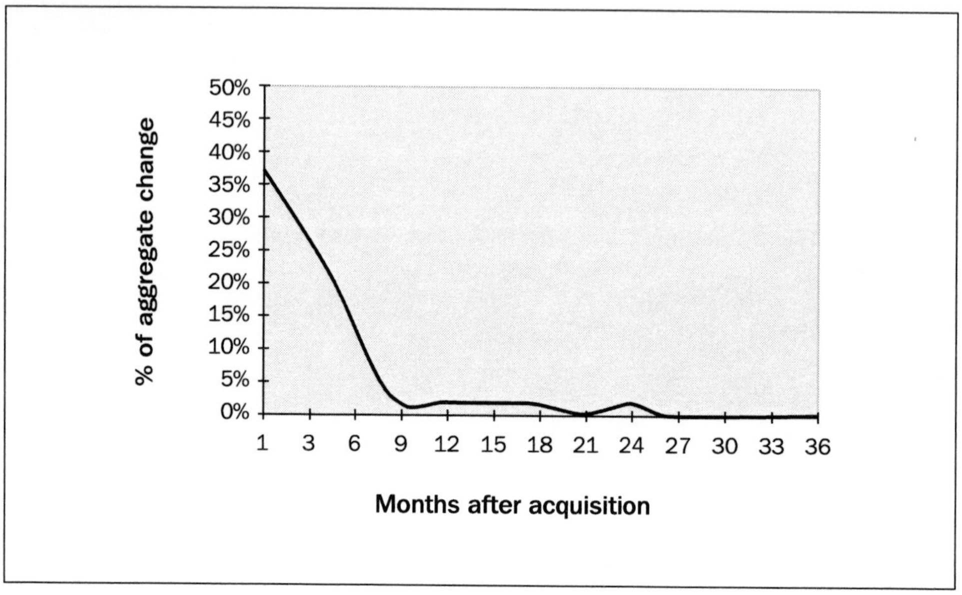

Source: Angwin (1998)

Whilst the term maintenance tends to suggests few adjustments, incumbents in fact view their altered circumstances as an opportunity for change. Figure 5.6 shows that most change occurs at the outset of the post-acquisition phase with 37 per cent of all new changes occurring in the first month. The level then declines sharply towards the ninth month where new changes continue at a low but sustained rate into the second year and beyond.

The speed of change at the outset of maintenance acquisitions is largely explained by the retention of Insiders who are capable of acting more rapidly than Outsiders. Insiders fully understand the business, have appropriate networks in place, and already have changes in mind at the acquisition date. They are spurred into action by the feeling that acquisition negotiations distracted them from managing their business. *'It takes your eye off the ball and you have to get back into the saddle'* (CEO of an acquired transport company).

As an *opportunity* for making changes, Insiders commonly use the general expectation of change amongst employees who anticipate aggressive, imposed changes by the acquirers. This gives the Insider a smokescreen for change. *'I had to get re-involved. I freely admit I made changes as quickly as I could as I knew what had to be done and I knew I could blame them on the new parent'* (MD of an acquired engineering business).

There is a cross-functional sequence in maintenance acquisitions of:

- financial changes; followed by
- management adjustments; and then
- operational changes.

Beyond this sequence it is difficult to discern a pattern amongst maintenance acquisitions, as they are far more focused upon exploiting their own markets than on 'accommodating' the new parent, whose advice is generally limited to financial reporting. Changes therefore tend to be business-specific rather than generic.

The long tail of change is a reflection of the difficulties faced in changing a successful company. The new parent may suggest ways, but these are likely to be perceived as harmful. As a rather rare Outsider in this context says of an acquisition in the medical sector,

> *Consultants have got to be in the top one percent of intelligence – they're deeply suspicious – ultra conservative – it took them twenty years to accept penicillin. They're powerful and can wreck change. I had to work very very slowly and very sensitively.*

Changes made in maintenance acquisitions

Maintenance acquisitions see the least amount of change of all the acquisition types. The main areas of change are in management and financial controls, which could be described as taking control actions. For the other dimensions of change, few actions are taken and, in general, change instigated by the parent is *vigorously* resisted.

Review top management

Maintenance acquisitions rarely see the removal of the managing executive. The retention of these Insiders is a clear indication of the parent company's faith in the quality of their purchase and its strategy.

Although maintenance acquisitions change the management team less commonly than the average for other post-acquisition styles, 40 per cent still do so. It seems that the acquisition gives the managing executive the opportunity to remove sub-optimal executives or those whose roles were duplicated at head office. Generally however, the managing team is clearly viewed as successful and so changes are fewer than in other acquisition types.

The management team often appears to have a bias for action after acquisition, perhaps in response to the need to bring the business back into line as well as a degree of optimism, although generally unfounded, about the support and resources that being part of a large group might bring.

Improve financial controls

All maintenance acquisitions are expected to conform with standardising group financial reporting and in many cases the managing executives feel the new formats are an improvement upon their own. To an extent this helps account for the high degree of acceptance. The main emphasis from the new parent is upon gaining financial information rather than just imposing controls.

Around half of maintenance acquisitions are controlled through financial budgets. This reflects a preference for acquiring companies to manage predominantly through the setting of budgetary targets. As the managing director of an acquired transport company says,

> *the budget is the bible. If we are keeping within budget, they don't interfere. They say, 'go ahead, run your business, you're the experts, we trust you'. When things go wrong, they get heavy.*

Characteristic amongst maintenance managing executives is the sense of a game being played where head office expectations can be manipulated and the acquisition portrayed in a favourable light. In the words of the managing director of an engineering firm, *'if you do your budgets the right way, then you've got a lot of flexibility'*. Achieving budget keeps head office at bay and *'if we perform, we get the investment. There's nothing better than just producing results'*. In addition to building in costs, maintenance managing executives often use *'cocoa tins'* or have *'something tucked up our sleeve'*.

Despite pressure from the new parent to bow to more rigorous controls, there is a strong sense of the acquired company defending itself from change either by game playing, saying the horse may learn to talk (see Chapter 2 : 27), or by more rigid stands such as not accepting budgets to the point of it being a resigning issue. An example is the managing director of a large acquisition in the communications industry:

> *If I had accepted what was being demanded then our investments would have been cut back, our customer service would have been cut back – everything would have been done for the short term.*

So whilst there is better financial reporting, there is a *tension* between what the parent company wants in terms of target setting and what the maintenance managing executive is prepared to accept. There is little doubt that their ability to produce results gives them the power to stand up for themselves in budget negotiations and helps generate trust. A common feeling amongst acquired CEOs is well illustrated by the CEO of a large acquisition in the communications sector:

> *We had a good track record both on our actual performance and on our budgets in the past so we were able to say, 'look, we know our business. These numbers are bizarre', and we rubbished the numbers.*

Change product market focus

Analysing product market position to uncover the possibilities open for management action is unlikely to occur in maintenance acquisitions. Few review their marketing plans as they feel they are already doing well. They do not alter their product market focus and only a minority focus on a specific market segment and product market items. Managing executives then are very comfortable with their markets and these are to be protected rather than altered.

Improved quality and service, and improved marketing

Echoing the above, maintenance acquisitions do not alter their approach to markets and customers and so only a minority make changes in terms of improvements to quality and service or marketing. Marketing operations are a sacred cow and indeed customers are to be protected from the new parent company.

Intensive efforts to reduce production costs

Maintenance acquisitions may see some tightening of production costs through improving labour productivity and plant capacity. This is a reflection of stricter financial controls and some investment in new technology.

In this area, the picture is one of incremental streamlining change rather than profound alterations. The managing executives vigorously defend their operations from parental intrusion. As the CEO of an acquired communications company remarked,

> *my major role throughout was defending the customers and the business from the owners.*

Reduction in debt

Maintenance acquisitions are financially strong and so a big drive to reduce debt or sell off assets is unlikely.

Problems with maintenance acquisitions

One of the critical features in maintenance acquisitions is the role of the Insider in protecting his business and customers from the new parent: *'fighting the corporate immune system'*. Related to this protective spirit is also a negative view of the new parent who is perceived to add little value to the acquired business. In the words of the CEO of an acquired communications company, *'the owners contributed absolutely nothing to the business at any stage'*. As a result, good corporate relationships are rare, Insiders are unlikely to influence head office, and the reason for them demonstrating good control of their companies is essentially to prevent interference from above.

This gulf between head office and managing executive is often exacerbated by the use of consultants by head office as this distances the acquired managing executive even further from decisions at head office. This lack of involvement makes him defensive so that: *'you make sure you convince the consultants that (the new idea) didn't apply to you'*. For the CEO of an acquired communications company, *'we fought like a dog with (management consultants) and, fine, we absorbed their methodology and used it to do what we wanted rather than what they came up with, silly ideas, because they didn't know the business'*.

This defensiveness is rooted in two issues: one, that the managing executive is in charge of a successful business which he intends to protect; and two, that the parent lacks understanding of the business and has a remote management style.

Most maintenance acquisitions highlight a lack of strategic direction from head office. Post-acquisition aftercare is also virtually non-existent. Despite the strategies that might have existed for the acquisition, there tends to be a gulf between group strategy and its implementation. Head office's divorce from operational reality becomes clear when, on the few occasions head office has taken initiatives, the lack of operational understanding has resulted in disaster with considerable resources and effort being consumed, unsuccessfully, in trying to solve technical mismatches.

Lack of understanding and apparent lack of interest from head office mean that managing executives will view any interest in the internal workings of their businesses as interference and as such it will be duly resisted. For this reason, managing executives will concentrate on producing results to avoid attracting negative attention.

The cost of this tension is an undermining of the real purpose of many of these acquisitions. In many cases the acquired company is admired and the parent believes it can learn from them. However, the barriers that are quickly thrown up can prevent this exchange from taking place. The intended influencing of the parent by the acquired company is rarely evident.

Case study 5.2

A maintenance acquisition

Utility PLC's acquisition of Micrometer PLC

Micrometer PLC was a very profitable, market leading, precision engineering company with several hundred employees. It was acquired[6] in 1991 by a major utility company, Utility PLC, who wished to keep the management. In the words of Andrews, the managing director of Micrometer, 'without management they were going to be a bit adrift'.

Post-acquisition there was a downturn in performance and a general malaise in Micrometer for four months due to uncertainty surrounding the new ownership and an enormous fear of change. Micrometer's staff felt the big corporate attitude would be 'we'll just close it'. 'Everybody expected a big wave of change but it never happened. Utility PLC didn't have anyone driving it.'

Post-acquisition, Andrews felt 'head office didn't know what their requirements were!' Apart from insisting that Micrometer adopt their reporting format within two months, and saying that costs should be reduced, 'they'd no clear pattern of what they were trying to achieve'. Whilst updating head office, Andrews was asked, 'Why do you just bring me problems?' He replied, 'I'm not bringing you problems, I'm telling you what's happening!' Indeed every business Utility acquired complained, 'What is the group going to do about this, and what is the group going to do about that?' to which Andrews replied, 'I've learnt that they're going to do nothing, so you bloody well get on with it and keep your head down.' 'Aftercare was non-existent.'

Head office did not drive change in Micrometer except to insist upon control of capital expenditure, parent financial reporting format, and to suggest cost reduction. Their managing of Micrometer consisted entirely of monitoring ever-more stringent budget requirements. In response, Andrews ensured that even during a difficult market, 'we've managed always to perform'. Achieving budget kept head office at bay and, provided the budgets were done in the right way, flexibility to match budgeted profit could be ensured.

Keeping a low profile has been a successful course of action. 'At the end of the day I decided to keep out of the way and let them carry on with the politics up there and just produce results; there's nothing better than just producing results.' Indeed Micrometer has consistently performed well post-acquisition. 'If we perform, we get the investment. If we don't perform, they'll come and dig around in it and we don't want that.'

Soon after the acquisition, Andrews took the initiative to make a few changes directly relating to the change in ownership. 'Because I had more time to spend on the business I had more time to identify what needed doing next and to drive it forward.' The finance director was retired and parent financial reporting welcomed as an improvement upon the previous system. An executive position which handled insurance and banking arrangements became superfluous as it duplicated a function in head office.

Andrews made further changes in response to the declining market. The changes 'weren't necessarily to do with the take-over. We were making changes because I thought it was appropriate to make changes.' These changes 'would have happened even if we had stayed private. Most changes are market driven.'

For Andrews, the worst part of the acquisition was his lack of involvement with head office which spent 'more time looking at things and doing nothing'. During the post-acquisition phase, head office was characterised by rare visits and remote decisions. They did not appear to have a sufficient understanding of what was going on in the companies. Andrews took action because he felt that if he waited for clear instructions from head office, 'I could have still been sat here. I haven't taken that tack because I believe that having taken the staff into a deal, I owed it to them to do the best for them.'

Being acquired by Utility PLC has allowed Micrometer to raise its business to the next level. There has been some limited nurturing with some capital investment in computer systems, although they could have paid for this themselves, and Andrews has been able to stand back to allow the management standard to rise. Andrews has been moved up to run a number of European businesses and there are now strong moves, some five years after the acquisition, to realise synergies with other group companies.

Maintenance acquisition summary

Maintenance acquisitions witness only a few changes as a direct result of acquisition. However, these tend to be less from the new parent and more from the acquired managing executive who views the acquisition as an opportunity to make changes that were difficult beforehand. In particular these changes focus upon senior management and tightening up of operations. These changes are generally incremental and intend to improve the business without transforming it. Other changes will be in terms of adopting parental financial reporting, improving controls and a degree of capital investment. Whilst there may be a promise of parental nurturing through investment, this is generally overstated.

In general, changes suggested by the new parent are fiercely resisted by acquired managing executives who, however, will make changes whilst responding continuously to alterations in their environments.

Whilst learning and organisational championing are desirable in maintenance acquisitions, the tensions thrown up by defending the business and managing short-term operating results present a significant obstacle.

Maintenance acquisitions: Main themes

- Low overall post-acquisition change:

    keep things as they are and preserve the core operations

    retain the managing executive

    the retained managing executive will defend the business from the parent.

- A bias for action to pull the business back into shape:

    adopt parental financial reporting system

    streamline management and remove the finance director

    tighten up costs of operations.

- Parental nurturing – although an anticipated benefit, this was limited and rare. Managing executives felt it was often paid for out of their own resources. Examples of capital investment tended to be in information technology/information systems.

- Learning is often cited as a major benefit but can easily be impaired by insensitive acquisition management.

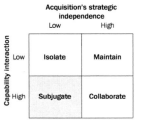

SUBJUGATION ACQUISITIONS

Subjugation acquisitions are about acquiring businesses in the same industry as the acquirer. The parent company has a profound knowledge of the industry and is generally trying to achieve synergies associated with economies of scale and scope. This is achieved by dismembering the acquired business and its complete integration into the parent group. The new parent is broadly clear on the changes it wishes to make so the main issues are to tighten up on the detail and to consider the implementation and timing. Subjugation acquisitions then experience therefore by considerable and sweeping change.

Timing of changes in subjugation acquisitions

Subjugation acquisitions are characterised by a burst of change at the outset, followed by a lull in activity during which there is an important planning phase, and then a wave of intense change. Thereafter there are clear diminishing subsequent peaks of activity at the 1 year mark and after 18 months.

| Fig. 5.7 | Subjugation acquisition – when changes start |

Source: Angwin (1998)

The waves[7] of change in subjugation acquisitions can be characterised as:

1 *Taking hold* of the acquisition – an immediate wave of change in the first month.

2 *Immersion* or planning stage – use of teams for 2–4 months.

3 *Major restructuring* – major changes around the 6 months mark.

4 *Reflection* – review of effect of changes around the 9 month mark.

5 *Secondary restructuring* – at the end of the first year.

6 *Consolidation* – reflection and further wave of adjustments up to 18 months.

7 *Refinement* – Fine-tuning.

Managing executives commenting upon such waves of change said: *'we had six months of causing difficulties, six months of realising them and six months of putting them right'* (finance director of an acquired food manufacturing business). *'At the end of the first year there was a taking stock of how well we had done, and a further rationalisation which was not in the plan and was completed in a further six months'* (director of a large communications acquisition). For the managing director of an acquired utilities company these subsequent waves were viewed as follows, *'after twelve months is a period of refinement and getting things done'*.

The taking charge activities in the first burst of change focus on:

■ communications

■ removal of corporate identity

- imposing financial controls

- senior executive change.

Whilst this is taking place, a **planning and consultation process** is set up to assess which areas are appropriate for change. In the words of a finance director of an acquisition in the food industry, *'we didn't know enough to go in there day one and suddenly do things'*. To better understand the acquisition, extensive use is made of integration teams, task forces, joint committees and parallel working. In essence, both businesses are run in parallel whilst evaluations are carried out on intended rationalisations. Planning and consultation takes up to two months: *'in about six to eight weeks we had blitzed it and worked out how we were going to operate the new district'* (Outsider at an acquired utility company).

This is a very sensitive time. Every effort must be made to:

- retain key operational staff and middle management

- motivate employees

- retain key customers

whilst at the same time assessing areas for rationalisation – an exercise in which acquired employees can make a substantial contribution.

Once the planning period is complete there is substantial change on many fronts, executed at speed. As the Outsider at a large media acquisition says, *'once the plans were complete, we incurred a redundancy bill and the wrath of lots of people and got on and did it'*. The main emphasis of change is upon de-duplicating activities. For instance, head offices and their functions, warehouses and depots, factories and other production facilities are rationalised often with heavy job loss. This activity is directly linked to a pervasive drive to reduce costs and many acquirers set themselves aggressive financial targets. Subsequent waves of activity tend to be remedial in nature resulting from the major planned restructuring wave of change.

Changes made in subjugation acquisitions

Removing acquired company corporate identity

In most subjugation acquisitions, where the acquired corporate identity is not synonymous with the product, it is removed very rapidly indeed – in many cases the acquirer aiming to achieve an 'overnight' change from 'old' to 'new' so that on day one of the acquisition, the acquired company looks and sounds new.

Corporate emblems and logos are changed, ranging from removing/destroying sculptures/monuments/flags to supplanting crests on office stationery. Signs will be removed from entry barriers and from over front doors, carpets with logos will vanish. Adverts will appear in the media to announce the change or, through reinvigorated product advertising, the new ownership will be subtly introduced – 'product x, now part of the y group'. Security guard uniforms will change with the introduction of new ties, cap badges and epaulettes. Receptionists, telephonists, secretaries will be 'sent to college' to learn the 'new greeting'. The spirit is very much, 'the King is dead, long live the King'.

Acquirers should not underestimate the impact of changing such symbols. Acquired employees identify with them in much the same way that army battalions and football teams identify with mascots and banners. In times of crisis, these symbols assume enormous emotional and psychological significance and their rapid change will be a big shock. This will be a big sign of a 'fresh start', but employees will also feel their loyalties being challenged as the majority are unlikely to have prepared themselves for the disruption of their psychological contracts. This uncertainty will feed and enhance their expectations of change.

The power and importance of employee attachment to symbols are well illustrated by the way that AT&T is reported to have dealt with the merger of two groups which had grown up in 'two very different business climates' (see Case study 5.3). Although the drama is perhaps more appropriate to the US, if the reader imagines himself in the place of the managers in the cameo, the 'shock' does demonstrate our unconscious emotional and psychological bonds with our company.

Case study 5.3

Importance of symbols – AT&T's approach to the merger of two groups

To release the managers from their psychological commitments to their 'old' group values, they were all led outside to where a wooden coffin awaited. To sombre funeral music, each of the 80 managers stepped up to the coffin, crumpled his or her worst case lists, letterhead, and business card and tossed them in. As the last manager stepped back from the coffin, the group was startled to hear a low, grumbling noise. Slowly a 100-ton paver rolled around the corner and headed straight for the group. At first, the managers stood paralysed, unsure of what was to transpire. But then the band broke into a rousing rendition of 'On Wisconsin', and the paver veered towards the wooden casket, flattening it and its contents of managers' worst case fears. Spontaneous cheering broke out among the executives as the paver rolled back and forth on top of the coffin.

Source: Mirvis and Marks (1992: 232)

Communications

Excellent communication is vital in subjugation acquisitions. It allows the acquired company to continue to operate effectively whilst task forces investigate areas for integration. Effective communications are needed to prevent the rumour mill from operating and the loss of the best staff. The fears of employees are well described by an Outsider managing director of a professional services acquisition, *'after every deal I have always met the staff and the things they always ask are, "What's the name of the company going to be? When are you changing the name of the company? Are you changing my commission plan? Are you changing my remuneration package? And will I still have the same manager?" – their world is in turmoil, they're all down to the bottom layer of Maslow, "how do I feed my family?".'* His advice is *'don't bullshit them. Don't commit to things you are not sure about. Be honest and open and be available'.* The other side of the coin is highlighted by the finance director of an acquired food manufacturing business: *'we didn't want people thinking, "well I'm going to be booted out" and then ruin our relationships with a couple of large supermarkets'.* The high priority given to communications is illustrated by the comments of the chief executive of a professional services firm acquisition, *'I visited every single office of both companies throughout this country in a three day period and spoke to as many staff as they could get in. As soon as it was done, I got to all the overseas offices as well. It was a major exercise.'*

Communications are not a one-off event or the repetition of a single message. As mentioned in the previous chapter, it is an ongoing, evolving process which is carried out through a range of mediums. Particularly in subjugation acquisitions, where there will be very substantial change, it is critical to maintain a stable workforce and this is greatly helped by flexible, responsive, accurate and honest communications throughout the entire integration period.

Review top management

Subjugation acquisitions see a great deal of change in the acquired top management team. Around 90 per cent of acquired directors are changed and some 75 per cent of managing executives are replaced. These executives are replaced as they are perceived to be a barrier to change and, in the case of changing the CEO, this symbolises change and the 'shaking of the tree' even if he is not seen to be a major obstacle.[8] In addition there may well be no senior positions available for them in the Group. In the vast majority of cases then, subjugation acquisitions will be managed by Outsiders who are generally associated with radical change.

The large number of changes in the management team is largely due to a number of positions being duplicated. Many subjugation acquisitions are characterised by a period of joint committees or 'parallel working' where opposite members of management work beside each other to assess which areas of the business should be rationalised and indeed how they should rationalise their own position. In one large communications acquisition by a competitor, there was an extensive use of joint committees and in a utilities acquisition, all executives had equal opportunity to apply for all the posts in the new integrated company.[9]

The general trend however seems to be the removal of senior executives and duplicate functions at the acquired head office rather than the removal of acquired operations management. As the finance director of an acquisition in the foods industry explained when justifying why the acquired board of directors was removed, *'the operational managers were the value and particularly the guys with the relationships with major customers'*. Consequently it is not surprising to see that 50 per cent of all acquired finance directors in subjugation acquisitions removed whereas marketing/sales directors fared rather better.

In a few instances, incumbents may remain in subjugation acquisitions, although as one remarked, *'if you're acquiring it's natural to put your guy in place'*.

Improve financial controls

In subjugation acquisitions, accounting and finance teams are the 'shock troops' of acquisition: *'our accountancy personnel went in there straight away'* (managing executive of a large communications acquisition). Financial controls assume a great importance in subjugation acquisitions as, through these controls, a common language is established, the acquired company understood, and areas for cost savings identified. Expressing the acquired company through the parent financial systems therefore assumes a high priority: *'Until you turn the lights on, you can't see where you're going'* (Outsider managing director of an acquired professional services firm).

Budgetary controls are seen as a vital part of controlling the integration activity and are of major concern at the outset of the post-acquisition phase. In the case of an acquisition in the food industry, the new CEO remarked that the first five months were spent *'agreeing budgets for the part of the activity that was going to be split into each of our three areas'*. The importance and indeed problem of focusing on coalescing accounts are shown in Case study 5.4, where priority is given to stitching accounts together and then assuming it will all work.

Change product market focus

The vast majority of subjugation acquisitions review the acquired company's marketing plan and, for many, the acquisition is driven by the wish to build market share in their own market. Post-acquisition changes are directed at achieving this aim by concentrating upon tight overhead control to reduce costs rather than investment. In particular, substantial efforts are made to gain improved terms and conditions from customers to achieve an immediate effect upon margins.

In subjugation acquisitions however, we do find that once the key customers have been secured, the extent of the effort focuses upon de-duplicating activities and rationalisations which means that the markets and the future can receive less attention than they deserve.

Improve quality and service

There is a general wish for most subjugation acquisitions to improve quality and service by reducing delivery days. This can be relatively straightforward and reduces costs quickly. There is also evidence of improving quality control and introducing after sales service, although these activities are less easy to achieve and often require investment before benefits show. Difficulties can be encountered in the area of promotions, such as price rebates, and special discounts where past practices may be poorly documented and/or complex. The emphasis however, in terms of quality and service, is generally to reduce costs and streamline rather than adding to service.

Improve marketing

Subjugation acquisitions see improvements in distribution channels, due to rationalisation, and there is an emphasis upon improving marketing information to the board. This betrays an inward looking perspective centred on marketing, rather than an outward focus on the customer. This is the danger that the CEO of an acquired communications company refers to when discussing an integration acquisition, *'it's difficult putting businesses together because you've got to spend so much of your effort facing inwards and so take your eye off the commercial football'*.

Intensive efforts to reduce costs

As one would expect with subjugation acquisitions, there are intense efforts to reduce production costs although this may not extend to making investment in new plants. The mentality is clearly one of cut back and reduce.

Many executives cite the drive for reduced costs to justify the price of the acquisition. In a very large acquisition of a communications business, a head office executive commented that, *'the price we paid required us to justify that price through overhead cuts. We had to deliver those overhead cuts and the very first thing we did, even before the deal was completed, was set up joint committees to oversee how costs could be reduced between the two organisations'*. The pressure to get costs down is evident in most subjugation acquisitions and is also apparent in Case study 5.4.

With an emphasis upon de-duplicating activities, overhead reductions are usually relatively straightforward to achieve. In particular, head offices and their staff are prime targets for rationalisation. As the managing executive of a utilities company remarked, *'it was obvious that we would only operate with one office and I'm sure somebody would have told me from on high if I'd said that we needed to keep two head offices going'*.

Reducing costs by de-duplication is foremost in the minds of subjugation managing executives. In many cases the rationalisation of assets is easy to achieve – as the managing director of an acquired utility company said, *'some of these decisions came out very easily once you gave them half a thought, because in one town, they had a depot, we had a depot, I mean it's as easy as that – you don't have two depots, you have one'.*

Substantial cost savings can also be achieved in the area of purchasing and supply chain management (PSM). McKinsey (1998) estimates reductions in costs may amount to 10–15 per cent of total cost of goods, and in an analysis of 50 recent mergers, suggests these savings can recoup at least half of the merger premium. The largest spending categories can be evaluated rapidly after acquisition by the use of several cross-functional teams, which often involves suppliers. Such cross-functional teams may also be able to help resolve issues of conflicting processes between organisations. Once cross-functional teams have evaluated the largest spending categories, the company should adopt the ambitious target of achieving most cost savings within the first 12 months of the post-acquisition phase.

Savings can come from increased bargaining power due to the larger size of the company, but in terms of management actions will require coalescing fragmented purchasing, introducing new suppliers, changing patterns of demand, devising creative strategies for negotiating contracts and closer involvement, in terms of better specification, with suppliers. Citing the example of the merger of two financial institutions, McKinsey (1998) shows that first year savings ranged from 8 per cent for ATMs to 20 per cent for credit reports and marketing brochures.

Substantial savings then are possible in the area of purchasing and supply chain management but are frequently not realised as the area often suffers from poor image and low expectations: *'historically, PSM has not been a breeding ground for top managerial talent'* (McKinsey, 1998). Many world-class companies have recognised that purchasing and supply management can be a source of competitive advantage and, as such, have elevated the status of the activity to a virtual line of business. To raise the profile of PSM as well as achieve substantial savings from the acquisition, it is critical to appoint a capable leader. However, acquirers should bear in mind that if there is a need to recruit such a person, it will probably take longer and cost more than expected.

Reduction in costs throughout the combined companies then is the primary driver in subjugation acquisitions. The main concern is how to extract such costs whilst keeping the operations running.

Reduction in debt

Often subjugation acquisitions make efforts to reduce the costs associated with the acquisition by selling off non-essential businesses. There can be a surprise here as the assets to be sold can be worth substantially more than anticipated. In Case study 5.4, part of the acquisition included three small businesses making poor returns. The finance director at the acquirer illustrated the mentality towards peripheral assets when saying, *'God knows what we're going to sell these businesses for. We don't know anything about them. And I think we more than tripled my estimate in terms of getting that back'*. The parent company managed to recoup some 20 per cent of the total acquisition cost.

Imposition of parent systems and structures

In all subjugation acquisitions there is a general sense of parent systems being imposed upon the acquired company. Upon being interviewed, some acquirers recognise a certain degree of arrogance in feeling that their systems were best: the 'conquering hero syndrome'. They also realise that many post-acquisition problems encountered are a direct result of their systems being inappropriate for the acquired business. For example, in one case, where the acquirer insisted on using its own warehousing systems instead of the acquired company's, the retained managing director described the difference as the parent company, *'selling drops for dollars whereas we were selling big chunks for a little less than dollars; trying to use their ideas in our warehouses gave us significant difficulties'*. Another example of parent companies imposing inappropriate views is drawn from the professional services industry. A regional structure was imposed upon an organisation that had previously operated on skill group lines. As the CEO of the acquired company remarked, *'what was realised later was that the right approach was the skill group approach and the regional approach was wrong'*. This was an error that caused human resources to suffer and *'the business has gone back now to a very much skill group and organisation based along skill group lines and not regionalised'*.

On occasion there may be a clear wish to take on board best practices in the acquired company. For instance, in the case study, the acquired company possessed a superior computer system to the acquirer. However it was felt that it would be far more expensive and difficult to change the acquirer's system than it would be to change the acquiree's system. In general where there were areas of overlap, and despite good intentions, the acquiring company's approach often won through. To an extent this may be due to 'arrogance' on the part of the acquirer, and in part it may be due to a lack of champions in the acquired company.

In the area of Information Technology it is also worth pointing out that there now appears to be a move, and it is certainly a major marketing pitch by Information Technology specialists in the banking sector for instance, to use acquisitions as an opportunity to change and homogenise all the computer systems. This is seen as preferable to spending large sums in adapting one organisation's technology to the other, which may already be beginning to date, and also takes into account the 'risk' factor that hidden incompatibilities may emerge to haunt the group.

Problems with subjugation acquisitions

Following the removal of the incumbent executive and corporate identity, there will be a great fear of change amongst employees. Indeed subjugation acquisitions are associated with very significant job losses. The fear of change leads to an 'us and them' culture which can be very obstructive. To an extent, this fear of change can be mitigated by excellent communications. The author is also aware of examples where hardships in the industry post-acquisition had a strong coalescing effect upon employees.[10]

Subjugation acquisitions are driven by a strong cost reduction mentality and the arrogance of the 'conquering hero syndrome' is hard to avoid. This can lead to errors in terms of sacking large numbers of people whose roles are not familiar to the parent company or whose value in the acquired company is somewhat different than conveyed by familiar job descriptions. Such people often carry important tacit knowledge which is then lost. For this reason, experienced acquirers have described middle management in the target company as the 'marzipan layer'.

Tacit knowledge can be overlooked post-acquisition; driven out by overfocusing upon codified knowledge. In subjugation acquisitions, companies often complain that although they kept all the documentation, they still encountered significant problems as they hadn't recognised that a lot of critical information is stored in employees rather than on paper. An example is where, in a large acquisition, the acquirer made every effort to keep pre-deal tax records but sacked the acquired company's finance department on day one. Unfortunately for them, the Inland Revenue has now taken a considerable interest in those tax records, the explanation for which is with ex-employees who are not minded to assist in these enquiries.

Most subjugation acquisitions experience disruption costs due to implementation difficulties. These are normally due to inadequate operational considerations, such as moving the major part of a factory only to find difficulties in selling the site, agreeing the importance of extending and modifying acquired operations but then finding it costs substantially more than anticipated, closing down a large regional production operation and encountering very strong union and local resistance, and a general unwillingness of many employees to relocate even such small distances as 8 miles![11] In continental Europe this issue of re-shaping workforces during implementation has been a particular difficulty for cross-border and domestic acquirers.[12]

It is worth suggesting that such expensive operational errors can be the result of a narrow financial approach to integration. As the case study will show, there is evidence that acquirers can assume that just by putting financial controls in place, the integration will be successful.

Beyond rationalisation

At the outset of subjugation acquisitions there is often the intention to harness the complementarity in the two firms once rationalisation is complete. This activity however is in marked contrast to harmonisation, as it involves capitalising upon differences. There is little evidence to support the notion that firms actually go as far as to harness complementarities and this may be because so much effort is expended upon harmonising the two operations. As a result, subjugation acquisitions generally create value through the rationalisation process as an end in itself rather than by focusing attention on harnessing complementarities.

Case study 5.4

A subjugation acquisition

Packers PLC acquisition of Edibles PLC

In the early 1990s, Packers PLC purchased Edibles PLC, a medium-sized, profitable food manufacturing business, as part of a sector rationalisation.

Whilst the negotiations had been handled by board members, the integration was managed by Keaton, finance director of a subsidiary – 'I had to say, "Well – what's going to happen?"'

There was a planning period of seven–eight weeks from when the take-over was agreed. 'We had been able to have a cursory walk around Edible PLC before the acquisition but we were not allowed to check it out fully. We had a gut feel that something would be closed but we couldn't be sure which factory.

'I was then parachuted in and we had a big meeting of managers and pushed out plans of activity for who's responsible for what. We overlaid a layer of management on top of their management and effectively we had people working side by side over that period of time. Their people were running the activity but if we wanted to influence them we did! We took the view, "Well, let's give ourselves a period of time during which, if people don't get on then guys will leave anyway, but we need to spend five months establishing exactly who the right people are. We know broadly the structure that we want, but let's create some interface between the organisations that allows us to start the planning process." Everybody knew that we were likely to do some rationalisation of factories and depots and we didn't know enough to go in there day one and suddenly do things.

'All the directors including the FD and the company secretary had gone except for one who we made managing director of one of the manufacturing operations and the directors of three small businesses remained, because we thought we were going to sell them anyway.

We don't want a board of directors floating around and I think they knew that. It was the operational guys that we might want to keep.

'We managed [Edibles PLC] as a separate activity' for five months and reported it separately in the management accounts. During that time, 'I went through the process of agreeing budgets in effect for the part of the activity that was going to be split into each of our separate areas'. Keaton then met with the managers who had spent two months ghosting the management and asked what they thought compared with the earlier ball park paper. In one business area 'people said, "It's going to cost us twice as much to build a bloody factory!" – great! In another they said "Oh fine, easy, we'll just integrate it. When can we start?"

'Before the end of the five month period we had already closed down one of their factories and moved the activity into our factory. Their factory was running probably at 60–70 per cent capacity whilst ours, three times the size, was running at 70 per cent capacity. You bang the whole thing in and it runs at 100 per cent capacity. So it just made sense. We incurred a redundancy bill and the wrath of lots of people and got on and did it.

'The five months really gave us time to completely get rid of every bit of identity that was Edibles PLC.' The head office was closed during the first five months. The period also gave them time to work out how to link computer systems together so that the financial reports could be produced without having a separate section for Edible PLC and 'so everybody understands how it fits together'.

'We had come up with a way during those five months that enabled us to understand who the good people were and who we wanted to keep and also we didn't get the people thinking well I'm going to be kicked out and therefore ruin our relationships with a couple of big customers which could completely destroy the rationale for doing the acquisition.'

As soon as the five month period was up 'a lot of people were banging tables saying we've got to get costs out. We ought to be able to run this lean and efficient. We don't have all those people, so we kicked them all out.'

There were some difficulties in removing so many people: 'what we didn't do was say, well they must be doing something.' As a result, a significant problem resulted in one factory and in terms of tax records 'the linkages from one record to another have effectively gone because they were within individuals' heads and those people have gone.

'Where things went wrong is we put it all into Packers PLC and then went, ah fine, it's part of Packers PLC now. We sort of stitched the accounting systems together, put somebody in charge of it and assumed it would work. And yes, it seemed to be fine for the first couple of months, but we are still having difficulty. Superficially we put the computers together to make them work. What we didn't do was to say, "well the computers are talking to each other, do the people? Are the people who are operating the computers talking to each other?" So we fixed the systems but we didn't fix the procedures.'

'I had to use all my persuasion and charm to get anything done. I was three grades lower than most people who I was getting to do things. I sat there face to face with three general managers and they're going, "Who's this idiot from head office?". I was sort of shuttling backwards and forwards as a diplomat rather than as a manager.' Keaton felt he needed a larger full-time team which would have speeded the process and been more comprehensive. 'There are a number of things lurking around that aren't absolutely critical but are now causing pains and difficulties because we didn't tie everything off as neatly as we could have done.'

Despite these problems, overall 'I think all the initial phases went reasonably smoothly because we understood the business – it was business that was familiar to us. We could talk the same language. We could plan it because we knew the things that would be issues.'

It is interesting to note in the case study that next to nothing is mentioned of customers, which shows the inward focus of management on handling the complexities of internal integration. In addition, the effort is entirely focused on reducing costs. There is no mention of how value might be 'created' in the future and instead there is an overwhelming sense that once all the cost cutting has happened then everything from the acquisition has been achieved.

Subjugation acquisition summary

Subjugation acquisitions are a true consolidation of two firms. Critical elements in achieving this are the appointment of an Outsider to lead the post-acquisition phase, a management team, excellent communications and numerous task forces to plan and then implement the rationalisation of the businesses. The identity of the acquired company is quickly removed as the acquired company is subsumed within the parent. Every effort is made to reduce costs and to move towards best practice. However, as pointed out above, best practice is often the acquirer's practice.

The main driver of change is to reduce the costs of duplicate operations. Often this is the overriding objective and it is no surprise therefore that in most instances subjugation acquisitions appear to be financially driven with insufficient attention given to operational issues. There are some occasional exceptions, such as where an incumbent managing executive remains to defend his operation. This is very unusual and does affect the integration process.

Once amalgamation has been achieved, there may be efforts towards developing and investing in differences. This, however, tends to be rare. The reason is that the identity of the acquired company has been erased and its 'champions' in senior management have often departed. Once the rationalisation is completed and cost reduction activities achieved, the acquisition is very often regarded as history.

Subjugation acquisitions: Main themes

■ Remove impediments to change:

   remove acquired company identity

   remove acquired management.

Continued

- Post-acquisition planning and assessment period:

  use of integration teams, parallel working, joint committees

  maintain morale whilst building understanding of business.

- High levels of change across the board, driven by cost reduction:

  de-duplicate activities with substantial job loss

  rationalise assets

  reduce operating costs

  impose parent systems.

- After major cost reductions have been achieved, consider how complementarities can be harnessed, rather than pursuing harmonisation at all costs.

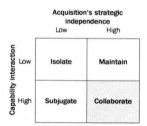

COLLABORATIVE ACQUISITIONS

In collaborative acquisitions, every effort is made to maintain the core of the acquired company whilst gently de-duplicating and investing to achieve substantial change in the enlarged group. There is clear attention to carrying out change in a very sensitive and careful way. The emphasis throughout is one of building through investment and mutual development. This is a more time-consuming process than acquisition styles such as subjugation and isolation discussed above.

It is very clear that the distinctive quality of this acquisition style is the deliberate effort to maintain and enhance differences between the two companies. These might be manifest in any area but our case study illustrates this in terms of product association, marketing and sales. A vital element of the process is the transfer of personnel, know-how and product design between the two companies to crystallise differences.

Maintaining differences is critical to the success of this acquisition style. Great importance is attached to preserving the characteristics and competencies of the acquired company. This is achieved by significant and highly visible investments. Great pains are taken to treat the acquired staff on equal terms with parent staff to engender a partnership atmosphere. Instilling confidence in the acquired company is paramount, and changes, other than initial investments, are subservient to achieving this objective.

This creation of a camaraderie and at least equal involvement of acquired employees, in task forces for instance, fosters a positive outlook towards change so that major changes can take place. The trust between the two companies at all levels is vital to enable significant transfers of resources between them in terms of employees, products and know-how.

Timing of changes in collaborative acquisitions

In terms of the timing of changes in collaborative acquisitions, there are clear differences from other acquisition types, with relatively low levels of activity at the outset of the post-acquisition phase. In the words of the managing director of a large acquisition in the food manufacturing sector, *'we did say at the outset that we were not going to come in and make wholesale changes'*. His explanation for taking this position was that *'there was a reluctance to change too much in what was a successful operation'* and he didn't want it unsettled. The contrast with other acquisition styles is made particularly well by the CEO of an acquiring manufacturing firm describing an exchange with the then incumbent chief executive of the target company. The latter remarked shortly after acquisition, *'well I suppose you've got a blueprint and within a week everything will have changed?'*. The former's comment was, *'we found this bizarre because we said, "no – we're not as presumptuous as to act like that, because we don't know your company", and the incumbent said, "well I can tell you, if we had acquired you,*[13] *within a week we'd know exactly what we'd be doing and it would have all changed", and we thought, there are two ways of doing it and it's not the way we're going to do it'*.

The issue of not wanting to disrupt the acquired company is clearly of paramount concern in this acquisition. As a result, *'changes went further down our calendar based on that judgement'*. Collaborative acquisitions are therefore characterised by the emphasis of change being delayed. There is a marked peak of change initiation at the six month point followed by a slump and then a resurgence towards the end of the second year. Although beyond the scope of Figure 5.8, changes often continue to be initiated for several years.

Fig. 5.8 Collaborative acquisitions – when changes start

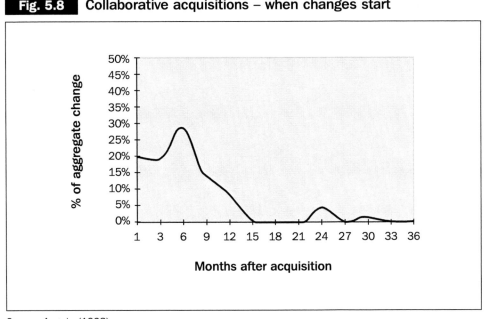

Source: Angwin (1998)

Change in collaborative acquisitions is more incremental than with other acquisition types. There is no great wall of change but rather an iterative form of interaction between the two companies. As the CEO of an acquiring food manufacturer remarked, *'we were alive to the dynamics of the situation. We actually changed a number of things as we went along. Rather than great directional changes, it was something that we felt could be done in the first year that we put off until the second year'.* He also suggested that the scale of change was affected by smaller changes than anticipated. This interaction meant longer time scales than for other acquisitions and *'those changes are still in progress (over four years on)'.* In addition, the iterative nature of the change process allowed changes to be handled in a sequential manner.

In many cases, collaborative acquisitions are still making changes through their iterative process. However as one managing director remarked, *'the future will not be presented as changes because we have two different companies; I think they will just be taken as changes within the group'.*

Changes made in collaborative acquisitions

Communications

Communications are vital in collaborative acquisitions. The key to success in this acquisition type is to earn and maintain employee trust and confidence as well as show that there is a future for their achievements.

Reviewing top management

The key to this acquisition style is the protection of the acquired company from uncontrolled intervention by the parent. Indeed, if anything, the emphasis should be the other way around – a sort of 'sweet shop' approach where the acquired company perceives the opportunities provided by its new parent and is able to select and value them in its own way. Understandably this can lead to frustration on the part of managers in the acquiring company who assume that, as their company has made the acquisition, they have superior rights and greater say in the future than acquired employees.

The top management team in the acquired company has a vital gate-keeping role to play in protecting the acquired company whilst allowing both companies to collaborate (Haspeslagh and Jemison, 1991).

Improving quality and service

These are often areas in which the acquired company is already strong. In the spirit of not damaging the value of the acquisition, few changes are likely to be made.

Improving marketing

The acquisition is often strong in marketing and so there is little reason to change this area upon acquisition. However, there will be a re-assessment of market position and it is likely that there will be some focus upon a particular market segment in which both companies can have an input. If this is an existing segment for both companies, then there will be efforts to re-negotiate contracts with customers and realise some scale economies as well as some potential economies of scope. As part of the re-assessment, there will also be an emphasis upon improving marketing information to the board.

Intensive efforts to reduce costs

In most collaborative acquisitions there is a duplication of resources. In value chain terms, **rationalisations** will most likely occur at the back end, in terms of plant and depot rationalisation for economies of scale, and in terms of support functions such as homogenising information technology systems.

Although these changes will occur over time, the critical factor is that this is not done hurriedly. This is a clear case of 'act in haste and repent at leisure'. Overly aggressive behaviour, whilst perhaps justifiably rational in the short term, i.e. getting costs down to repay acquisition premiums, will be very expensive in the medium term by sending the wrong message to acquired employees and so undermining the strategic purpose of the acquisition. As a result, changes may well be deferred rather than damage the spirit and purpose of the acquisition.

More than any other type of acquisition, collaborative acquisitions are associated with **investment** to reduce costs. In particular there is often investment in and the adoption of new processes as well as plant and machinery. It is very unlikely that control of production costs will be tightened or overheads reduced as these areas are likely to be well managed already, and perhaps more importantly, this would go against the spirit and purpose of the acquisition style.

Investment will not be limited to focusing just on reducing costs. It is particularly important in collaborative acquisitions for re-establishing confidence amongst acquired company employees as well as beginning to build the sense of partnership between the companies. At a later stage in the integration, investment is used to enhance differences between the two companies.

Reduction of debt

Collaborative acquisitions are likely to be in reasonable financial health prior to acquisition and to have been well run. For this reason, focusing upon reducing debt is likely to be of a low priority.

Transfer of resources

Transfers between the companies are important to achieve added value. However, such transfers need to be carefully handled to avoid any corrosive effects. Collaborative acquisitions see substantial transfers between the two companies as products, personnel and know-how are polarised to give maximum differences at the front end of operations. These transfers take place over a considerable period of time.

Problems with collaborative acquisitions

The main challenge with collaborative acquisitions is to build trust in acquired company employees whilst educating acquiring company employees that they are on an equal footing in the enlarged group with acquired employees and that some are not more equal than others. The early stages of the acquisition are critical for establishing the right atmosphere for this integration style and so problems will consist of actions, which may seem innocuous, or the imposition of standard procedures in an unthinking way, which may be inconsistent with building trust. In particular, the acquirer's managers may quickly begin to impose upon the acquired company which will quickly result in barriers being raised.

It is not enough to refrain from actions that may damage trust, as problems will occur if the acquisition is left in something of a vacuum. There needs to be positive action to reinforce the message. However, whilst investment can send the right message, rather like the Victorian gift ethic it can be misinterpreted as a sign of superiority, ownership and lack of self-determination.

Building trust and so preventing the erosion of the acquisition's distinctive qualities will mean controlling and even holding back the pace of change and realising that quick wins can be damaging. Potential difficulties can arise for top executives who may need to manage conflicting expectations from shareholders who adopt a short-term position and from the management of an acquisition style which suggests longer time frames.

Case study 5.5

A collaborative acquisition

Fortress PLC acquisition of Homeland PLC

Fortress PLC, a food manufacturer, acquired Homeland PLC, of the same industry, during a wave of sector consolidations.

Vaughan, corporate development director of Fortress prior to the bid, was appointed CEO of the acquisition when the board of Homeland resigned shortly afterwards. 'With the board leaving, we discovered that they had not been running the company, but their corporate position in the marketplace. The good news for us was there was a level below that who were effectively running the company and running it very well. We were not going to come in and change them, we were going to let them be their own masters.' However, 'in press terms, it had been a hard fought acquisition and the confidence of the management team was badly shaken. It was very important for us to maintain the establishment and the morale. If you cannot succeed in giving that confidence, then you run a very high risk of losing folks. We actually lost only one senior manager, and he left for personal reasons, which is astounding.'

Vaughan said he 'was able to develop a spirit, a camaraderie and an approach that this take-over isn't a bad thing – where are the benefits we can get out of it? Let's not be the wounded hurt little company that's been acquired by this large bidder because we're prouder than that – let's show how well we can make it work.'

The previous management team 'did not spend money'. 'One of the very first things changed was, we completely renovated the office block, because it was the pits – there were literally buckets on the floor to stop water coming in. It was an investment, a big sign.' Vaughan believes he 'would have spent five times that looking back, because it was a very, very important signal'. He also instigated a training programme and actually saw improvement. 'We didn't come down and say, you will do training in x, y and z. We said, there is a training programme in place – come and tell us what you want.'

There was clear evidence of engaging staff from both companies to drive changes forward. 'We were, always, always aware that we should balance the team across incumbents from the two businesses. It got people closer together and it showed they were equals in the project and we were at pains to make sure that a certain number of projects were led from one side of the company and an equal number from the other.'

In terms of the major changes, 'we fairly quickly separated the sales and marketing and commercial activities of both companies away from the production capabilities and resources of both companies. We set up three divisions: a Homeland sales and marketing division, a Fortress sales and marketing division, and we took out manufacturing, production, stock holding, warehousing, from both companies and combined them into a central division which was our manufacturing and operations division. We decided that the area where more synergies could be achieved, but could easily be sold to both management teams, was in manufacturing and production.' One of the Fortress manufacturing plants was closed down and, with a substantial capital injection, the Homeland plant was able to take on the additional volume.

Vaughan increased the focus of the sales and marketing parts by stopping Fortress's involvement in the volume business and by transferring those activities into Homeland. In return, the development potential brands in Homeland were transferred to Fortress which had considerably more experience and presence in this area.

'We wanted to give a very strong signal that we were keeping these companies separate. By transferring the skills and expertise and type of business from one company to another, which we were saying fitted better in one than the other, we felt that, although not always the best way to run the business, it was a very clear demonstration that there were two separate operations here, which gave a degree of confidence and commitment to the people who were in both companies.'

The Information Technology system at Homeland needed replacement and so the IT system was reengineered for both companies. 'It would have been wrong of us to say that we have an all singing, all dancing IT system and dump it on Homeland. One sees companies who say, "well the new company will just run our systems". I know we didn't do that. I'm glad we didn't do it and I think we were smart not to do it. We designed it with both companies in mind. I took the advice of my (Homeland) management team on what we needed to make it run and what wouldn't help it run.

'In year three we started looking seriously at the transfer of people. We've always been very, very aware that the danger is that the acquiring company – it's all of their guys who get the jobs. Now, if anything, if there is a slight imbalance, it's probably in favour of the acquired company. We acknowledged that you could as well be an expert IT person in one company as the other.' It was slightly more difficult on the sales side, 'but I'm not saying it's impossible to transfer because we have transferred a number of folks.

'I would judge the deal in terms of continuing development of companies, continuing profit development, the retention of the right staff, the development of the business, the retention of the customer base, our efficiency levels, our cost base. On all those things we have more than achieved.'

Summary of collaborative acquisitions

A critical facet of collaborative acquisitions is to maintain the distinctive qualities of both companies and to enhance differences. An important element of this process is the transfer of personnel, know-how and product design to crystallise differences.

Maintaining the characteristics and competencies of the acquisition is achieved by significant and highly visible investments as well as taking great efforts to treat acquired staff on equal terms with acquirer staff to develop a partnership atmosphere. Instilling confidence in the acquired company is paramount, and changes, other than the initial investments, are subservient to achieving this objective.

In this context, the use of integration teams can lead to camaraderie and foster a positive outlook towards major changes. This also enables significant transfers of resources between companies.

Change clearly takes on an iterative quality in a reciprocal acquisition with joint teams and equal input. In the words of Vaughan, *'we were alive enough to the dynamics of the situation. We changed a number of things as we went along'.*

Collaborative acquisitions: Main themes

- Maintain distinctive characteristics in the acquisition:

  establish a gate-keeping structure to protect the acquisition.

- Build trust in the acquirer and work towards partnership:

  establish joint working parties

  invest in the acquired company

  avoid changes which could erode confidence in the acquisition.

- Transfer resources to create value:

  use resource transfer to crystallise differences

  beware of the corrosive effects of rapid resource transfer.

- Recognise the dynamics of the collaborative style:

  be prepared to adjust plans to reflect the iterative nature of the style

  expect a long time frame.

- Defend the style against pressures for more immediate results.

THE NATURE OF THE MANAGERIAL CHALLENGE

Each acquisition type presents a quite different managerial challenge (see Table 5.2).

Table 5.2 Managerial challenge of each acquisition type

Acquisition type	Managerial challenge
Subjugation	Need to change everything, at the same time, in a very short time scale and the changes are interrelated.
Collaborative	Fundamental change is needed in both organisations without creating barriers. There has to be substantial transfer of resources to create value and yet it is critical to preserve both core competencies.
Isolation	Rapid substantial change with severely constrained scope for action.
Maintenance	Making improvements without damaging the acquisition or raising barriers to learning.

Subjugation acquisitions also see high levels of change, but these are not carried out immediately. There are substantial interdependencies between the organisations to be managed and this requires a complex approach necessitating careful planning and the use of task forces to accommodate the higher information needs. Everything must be changed rapidly but all the parts affect each other. Here the emphasis can be said to be doing things differently and there is a mutual interaction between the newly acquired company and its parent. On completion of a subjugation acquisition, both organisations will have changed, unlike the isolation or maintenance acquisitions, which will be still clearly identifiable.

Collaborative acquisitions also see longer time scales for change and it is important to consider dependencies between and within several components. These connections are explicitly recognised and managed sequentially. Change therefore focuses upon specific components in turn. There is an explicit interaction between the new parent and the acquired company in carrying out changes which occur in both organisations. Although these changes take place over a long period of time, the outcome is for fundamental change in both organisations.

Isolation acquisitions are also about doing the same things better and acting rapidly, although the scale of change is substantial. Time is short, requiring concerted action, but there is a limit to resources which severely constrains the scope of action in the acquired company. Often held in hermetic isolation, to avoid contaminating the parent group, isolation acquisitions focus upon a number of key changes. These are acted upon very rapidly, in an attempt to restore the business to good health and also win the confidence of the new parent.

Maintenance acquisitions see low levels of change which are piecemeal in nature and contained within the acquired company. The changes are aimed at improving what is already being done and there is an aversion to doing things differently. In the eyes of the managing executives, the changes are not perceived as changes at all, but simply differences in the way things are done. Indeed, most of our interviewees said that the new parent did not specify any direction and so they continued to find their own way, reacting to changes in their markets.

In summary, we can see four distinct managerial challenges in these acquisition styles. These challenges revolve around the speed with which change should take place, the amount of change needed, and the level of interaction with the new parent company (see Figure 5.9).

Fig. 5.9 **Characterising approaches to change by acquisition type**

		Volume of change		
		High	Low	
Timing, emphasis of major change	Immediate	**Isolation** Focused change	**Maintenance** Piecemeal change	Running the same company better
	Delayed	**Subjugation** Complex change	**Collaboration** Sequential change	Changing the acquired company to do things differently

Notes

1 We pointed out in Chapter 2 the difficulties SmithKline Beecham encountered in being perceived to move too slowly in this regard.

2 The turnover rate of top management is significantly higher than for control companies and, in an investigation of 102 target companies, 77 parent companies and 75 control companies, this difference has been shown to be most pronounced in the two years after the deal (Walsh and Ellwood, 1991).

3 In terms of statistical differences, most were in operations, followed by marketing.

4 Figure 5.5 does not show the *duration of change*.

5 Although such groups are not conglomerates, their performance and control systems force managers to act as though they are, so talk of synergies between businesses is perceived by the managers as a threat to their own autonomy and performance.

6 Actual bid size has been disguised to protect the identity of the company.

7 Whilst the waves are apparent in this type of acquisition, the timing and duration will be affected by the size and complexity of the businesses.

8 To some extent the CEO provides a scapegoat suggesting the past was inadequate.

9 Although in this case, their laudable stance had to be adjusted to senior and middle management as the sheer logistics of interviewing every member of staff for every position began to overwhelm the integration.

10 Indeed, in the US crises are known to have been engineered by the acquiring management to achieve this end (c.f. Pettigrew, 1985).

11 Top and middle management often forget that employee attitudes to jobs are less singular than their own, with strong local social/cultural ties meaning more than salary increases and/or promotions.

12 In continental Europe the issue of redundancies is far more contentious than in the US or UK and indeed is responsible for the failure to close a number of large mergers. Employment legislation makes it very difficult to reduce workforces and, as restructuring is a major source of post-acquisition value, can thwart acquirers' attempts to make the new group work.

13 It's worth noting that two years earlier the acquired company did have aspirations to acquire the new parent.

6

Not-for-Profit mergers

INTRODUCTION

Not-for-Profit organisations are under increasing pressure to merge. What are the problems and processes that face such organisations? In this chapter we shall examine, in brief, the pressures upon such organisations to merge, suggest reasons why merging can be particularly difficult and, through the use of examples in the higher education sector, show particular areas requiring the attention of the practising manager.

The term 'Not-for-Profit' (NFP) embraces a very wide field of organisations from the monopolies of state run services, such as the emergency services, health service, tax authorities, customs and excise, to non-state funded local establishments. Most NFPs rely upon a multitude of funding sources to support their activities. Such groups include charities, religious groups, the educational sector (schools, colleges, universities), theatres, museums.

In recent years such organisations have been going through significant upheavals. Regulatory changes in the UK since the 1980s, and growing incursions of market pressures, have resulted in organisations having to face a different funding balance and respond to more direct market pressures. One sign of these pressures has been the rise in mergers and acquisitions.

The underlying ideology and values of stakeholders are of central strategic significance to NFP organisations. NFPs are more dependent than profit oriented businesses upon funding from their sponsors, users are separated from providers, and employees are not separable from the organisation's service. Although there is a strong move by many of these organisations to adopt some of the features of profit oriented organisations – witness the transfer of entrepreneurial business talent across this boundary – these differences pose special difficulties in terms of NFP mergers.

REASONS FOR POST-MERGER DIFFICULTIES IN NFP ORGANISATIONS

Complex and competing stakeholder voices

NFP organisations have a different and perhaps more complex set of stakeholder influences than profit oriented companies. Whereas the latter have a broadly singular objective in maximising return to shareholders, with which their stakeholders are generally aligned, in NFP organisations there are likely to be multiple and competing perspectives. Major influences are generally from the fund providers who may, amongst themselves, view the NFP organisation in different ways. Although not fund providers, employees are also an important voice as they are not separable from the service provided. Service users may also have different perspectives, although where they do not contribute much revenue, their voice is likely to carry less weight than other groups.

Funding

The need for funding then can lead to the strategy of the organisation focusing upon resource acquisition rather than its intangible outputs. This separation is emphasised by fund providers often not being the direct beneficiaries of the service – so that money for new buildings may be raised, but not for running them. In addition, funding is often supplied in advance of the services being offered, such as grants for instance. This means that fund suppliers have considerable power and influence over Not-for-Profit organisations, whereas 'users' have considerably less power than with profit oriented companies.

An example of the relative difference in power can be found in the high influence of the 'providers' of funding for the National Health Service, and the relatively low influence of the 'users', i.e. the patients.

As funding can be derived from a wide range of bodies, it is not surprising that these multiple sources lead to different objectives and expectations from sponsors. This can lead to considerable political lobbying and difficulties of clear strategic planning, as top management will always be alert to a sponsor's views of organisational activity.

When resources become constrained, the balance of funding may need to move towards commercial ends which can conflict with the mission of the organisation. For instance, a cathedral's mission is about charity and worship which is contrary to charging admission and having large numbers of tourists in the building.

In competing for external funds, NFP organisations can become overly concerned with efficiency rather than service quality – in other words, strategies oriented more to sponsors than to employees and customers. This tends to result in drives for increased efficiency and is often perceived as an intrusion in the organisation's internal management.

Inseparability of employees and service

In NFPs, at the group and individual level, values and beliefs are very deeply rooted. They are an integral part of the service offering and are reflexive in nature so that attempts at change are likely to be strongly resisted on the grounds of damaging the spirit and purpose of the organisation. These values and beliefs are bound up in issues of 'professionalism' and 'legitimacy'.

Many NFP workforces can be viewed as 'professionalised' in terms of what they do. Professionalism consists of two dimensions: (1) a structure, which includes a code of ethics, rules of entry, exams; and (2) attitudes, which is the right to practise in the way they see fit, and not be imposed on from outside. Professionalism is an occupational strategy, a strategy of control and self-regulation, a strategy which excludes outsiders. Examples of highly professionalised workforces would be in medicine and the law.

Professionalised workforces have their own standards and views on legitimacy. Change imposed from outside the profession would therefore appear 'illegitimate', as it would conflict with professional autonomy and control, and be resisted. An example from a doctor in the Health Service: *'it's all very well to keep on about reducing costs, but what about the quality of the service?'* Professionalism and its service ideology form a major barrier to change.

When resource constraints begin to put pressure upon beliefs, individuals and groups will tend to retreat into the core of those values in defence. It is this self-reinforcing nature as well as the intangibility of such values that present a major obstacle to change. An example of resource constraints surfacing underlying values and leading to a defence based upon beliefs can be seen in the church. Diminishing income and attendance have led to practical questions over the wisdom of maintaining large numbers of costly buildings. Whilst the economic case seems clear, to practitioners of the religion, buildings are defended as far more than just housing for the organisation. They possess enormous spiritual, ceremonial and symbolic significance. In other words, a policy to close down such buildings calls into question the very nature of religious practice and value, for every aspect of the way in which religion is conducted is viewed as critical to its nature and its 'strength' is in its constancy. It is ironic, then, that as the 'historical and symbolic wealth' of a church building tends to increase with age, its practicality often diminishes as the costs of maintenance rise. The strength of an ideology in its practice may be its weakness, as self-reinforcement in times of change builds resistance to effective adaptation.

Forces for merger

Whilst many cases are made for merger, to achieve scale benefits for instance, the reality is that mergers are very rarely driven internally by institutions, but by *external pressures*. One reason is that NFPs allow conflicting agendas to operate under one umbrella. When resources are plentiful, different agendas can coexist. However, when resources become constrained, stakeholder agendas, rather than coming into alignment, are more likely to become less tolerant of the positions of others. A single coherent voice for making a merger is very unlikely to emerge.

The pressure for merger, then, comes from external sponsors. Their external pressure is essential for overcoming the natural resistance to change, which will surface with market interventions, in these institutions. For many NFPs this pressure may be manifest in the reduction in public funding and changes in legislation. In sectors where such pressure is already being felt, NFPs are becoming more managerial, with more directive management and the gradual introduction of methods and measures more commonly seen in the private sector. Such change is beginning to create opportunities for more entrepreneurial initiatives in terms of institutional advancement.

Whilst external pressures may force the trustees of organisations, for instance, to initiate merger talks, the depth and feeling behind each organisation's values, embodied in the employees, make the possibilities for agreeing a merger difficult. Indeed, it seems more common to hear of talks being called off amongst NFPs rather than leading to a deal. An illustration of the difficulties is provided by the discussions which surrounded New York University's merger with Mount Sinon Medical Centre (see Case study 6.1).

Case study 6.1

New York University's merger with Mount Sinon Medical Centre

There was considerable rancour between the doctors who felt that their departments would lose out in the combination. The trustees tried to continue the talks, whilst the doctors formed a 'Committee of Concerned Physicians' which held secret meetings, distributed unsigned leaflets containing inflammatory language and raised $40,000 to mount a legal campaign against the merger. The talks collapsed, but were later re-opened quietly with less involvement from the doctors.

Source: Derived from *The Wall Street Journal*, 21 Nov 1997

One can only speculate how well an integration of such institutions would proceed if these talks succeed. The example however does show how the trustees are responding to external forces threatening the economic viability of the institution, whilst employees, acting as the guardians and enactors of the institution's core values and beliefs, fear the merger will compromise the spirit and purpose of the organisations, in this case, achieving educational excellence.

DIFFICULTIES IN NFP MERGERS

In the US, mergers were seen as a panacea for troubled hospitals. By combining a couple of major NFP facilities, the resulting institution should be capable of withstanding competing pressure from managed care and anticipated Medicare cuts.

The reality is that some of these merged hospitals are now losing more money than ever. Cost cutting drives have stalled and staffs feud (see Case study 6.2).

Case study 6.2

Blending Beth Israel and Deaconess anaesthesiology departments

The Beth Israel Deaconess Medical Center in Boston is expected to lose $50m this year. The intention was to blend two clinical units, but after one and a half years of arguing, despite using high profile mediators, the attitude remained, 'I will kill you rather than join you'. In the end, the Deaconess anaesthesiologists resigned en masse,[1] and the remaining Beth Israel crew run back and forth between the two facilities.

Source: The Wall Street Journal, 14 May 1999

In common with mergers in the profit oriented sector, there are bound to be issues of personal egos and opportunism. However, in the NFP sector employees are imbued with a set of values and practices which are distinct and self-reinforcing. Even the smallest changes are seen as an assault upon core values. For instance, in the merger in Case study 6.2, even the suggestion of moving the start time of operating-room schedules by just 15 minutes required weeks of negotiation. In the words of Mark Wietecha, a consultant for Kurt Salmon Associates in Atlanta who worked on the merger, *'making these consolidations work is like going through Dante's inferno'* (*The Wall Street Journal,* 14 May 1999).

MERGERS IN HIGHER EDUCATION

Forces for merger

Since the mid 1970s there has been an increasingly critical and questioning attitude by successive governments toward public spending on higher education. This heightened political concern about costs and effectiveness, as well as gradual increased exposure to market forces during the 1980s, has led to an increasingly managerial approach to the operation of higher education, has focused attention upon institutional patterns and raised the possibilities for greater organisational effectiveness through mergers. In the abstract, growth through mergers offers many advantages including economies of scale through overhead reduction per student, and the possibility of greater funding resources with which to meet the increasing costs of research in science and technology.

Obstacles to merger

Whilst there appears to be a clear economic case for mergers, there are significant obstacles. Universities have generally tried to be all things to all people in offering a wide, balanced range of subjects at a highly specialised level. There is also a strong pecking order amongst institutions based upon research performance, attractiveness to students, ability to earn from industry. Employees are likely to have strongly held views on the institution's particular balance in these areas and, as significant stakeholders, will have a strong influence upon the success of merger talks. In addition to the issues of the spirit and purpose of the institution, and its reputation, in the UK geographical proximity is also important for economies to be realised.[2]

Finding appropriate merger partners then is very difficult due to ingrained attitudes and beliefs within organisations and the small pool of neighbouring candidates. Indeed, spatial proximity appears to be positively related with the number of mergers that have taken place in the higher education sector (Rowley, 1997).

Triggers for merger

Triggers for merger in higher education have increased (see Table 6.1). Reduction in government funding, reduced student numbers, a changing market for different styles of courses have raised question marks over increasing numbers of institutions in terms of their viability.

Table 6.1 Factors stimulating mergers in higher education

Internal drivers	External drivers
Desire to concentrate academic, personnel, and financial resources	Decline in the number of traditional 18 year old students
Desire to adjust academic profile and market niche	Reduction in government funding
Desire to diversify existing degree programmes in response to widening markets	Search for new, alternative sources of funding
Ambitions to improve status in institutional rankings, nationally and internationally	Change in markets, such as the greater demands for part-time and modular courses to attract mature and non-traditionally qualified students
Desire to achieve economies of scale, such as through common library, computing, or purchasing services	Rise of publicised league tables and greater market competition

Source: Adapted from Temple and Whitchurch (1994)

Negotiations

Critical issues during negotiations are:

- differences in institutional culture
- academic quality and reputation
- relative size
- leadership styles and management structure
- location.

Differences in institutional culture

Core to the institution are its beliefs, aspirations and expectations. These are embodied in the academic staff who are part of the 'product' of the institution and not easily replaced. They are highly sensitive to potential change in the spirit and purpose of their institutions and negotiations will depend upon the merger building and enhancing core beliefs rather than eroding or compromising them. An example in higher education would be the furore over the future of the tutorial system at Oxford University in the face of potential reductions in government funding. Many Oxford academics argue that it is an essential part of Oxford education, whilst the economic case for large 'grandstand' style lectures is clear to see.

Whilst issues such as job security and career opportunities are important tangible issues, and indeed the issues upon which advisers concentrate, employees in the NFP sector generally give greater weight to other values. Their motivation is far more dependent upon intangible values and for a merger to work depends upon them buying into such intangibles.

Academic quality and reputation

Institutions are highly conscious of their quality, not least because it is linked to funding. Any merger needs to consider the likely effect upon rankings. Rather than attempting to build upon existing strengths, many mergers have sought to broaden their offerings. This may enhance academic position, and create new opportunities for dynamics between different subject combinations, or a more highly specialised approach to certain areas.

Relative size

There is always the risk that a small institution may be swallowed by a large one, or that two equally sized institutions will end up paralysed. However, it may be more useful to consider some of the differences more closely (see Tables 6.2 and 6.3):

Table 6.2 Similar sized institutions with similar subjects

Institutional level	Sub-institutional level
How will similarities be fused?	Is there duplication or complementarity between aspects of the subject taught at undergraduate level?
	What are the research interests of staff?
There is likely to be an issue of staff morale with fear of rationalisation	
There will be issues of linkage between academic complementarity and physical location	

Source: Derived from Palfreyman, Thomas and Warner (1998)

Table 6.3 Dissimilar sized institutions with similar subjects

Institutional level	Sub-institutional level
Senior management need to make a judgement about the quality of provision	
How will similarities be fused?	Complementarity at the sub-department level?
	What are the research interests of staff?
There is likely to be an issue of staff morale with fear of rationalisation	
There will be issues of linkage between academic complementarity and physical location	

Source: Derived from Palfreyman, Thomas and Warner (1998)

Where the institutions have dissimilar subjects, success will be determined by the degree of dissimilarity and the opportunities for future integration.

Leadership styles and management structure

Power bases within institutions, such as research groups, departments and management teams, can lead to very complex and unwieldy decision making. External pressure is often needed to overcome difficulties and the move towards a more managerial stance may also help to promote change.

In the merged organisation there is also the difficulty of selecting which individuals will hold key posts and what will happen to those where there is no equivalent post. This issue is most pronounced where institutions are of different sizes.

Location

The location of campuses has implications for the management of the merged institution. Geographical configuration must align with the style of senior management, coherence in curricula and balance between central control and devolved structures. Where the merger is driven by meeting some external criteria of size, separate campuses can remain but may later become a force for disintegration, whereas the potential for fuller integration, benefits and coherence may result from geographical proximity (Palfreyman, Thomas and Warner, 1998).

Integration considerations

Palfreyman, Thomas and Warner (1998) raise a number of important issues for consideration when embarking upon merger integration. These form the basis for Table 6.4.

Table 6.4 Issues for consideration amongst higher education mergers

Symbols	The new name can cause bitter dissension as it is a symbol of relative importance to employees.
Future role of the CEO	Complexity of the issue often underestimated by appointing committees CEO must: ■ have vision ■ be able to get employee buy-in ■ be able to put infrastructure in place.
Academic integration	Increased scale: ■ curriculum revision for more courses ■ wider range of supervisors at doctoral level ■ strength in depth for research ■ spreading administration load ■ collaboration on income generation ■ enhanced flexibility on fund allocation for equipment and facilities. Balance Need to identify academic interests to ensure 'value added' Are weaknesses countered?
Estate	Rationalising estate can bring significant financial advantages and should occur rapidly. However, there may be important third party links to consider:

- helps to establish the new identity of the institution
- helps to break down barriers between staff.

Consolidation of estate can lead to significant problems as buildings and previous location can have strong local and institutional associations.

Multi-site institutions can result in significant administrative difficulties, e.g. a head of department has to manage his operation at several sites and needs to liaise with a remote head office.

Structure

Departments may easily fit into existing structures.

Departments may not have a natural home and will then form a self-contained entity. This means old set-ups may remain and not be integrated. Whether this matters will depend upon the new mission and top management values.

Support services

To what extent can these (library, shops, facilities) be centralised?

What systems are appropriate?

Will growth in student numbers affect systems?

Administration

Student records will need to be integrated, credit systems reviewed, degrees standardised, regulations amended, prospectuses and advertising revised.

Boards

Appropriate Boards need to be set up rapidly.

Members of staff need to feel that they are contributing as soon as possible.

Curriculum

Arrangements for students currently on programmes?

Development of new programmes/options?

Research planning

Effect upon RAE ratings?

In equipment intensive areas, decisions will need to be made about expansion of teams or amalgamation of interests.

Personnel

Academic personnel need to buy in as they are part of the product (sometimes 'no detriment' clauses are used to assure staff, but these can handicap restructuring).

Expectations need to be managed through clear communications and supported by appropriate actions. Morale can be affected by minor issues such as delay in pay, poor communications etc. In a merger of equals, physical equality is as important as academic integration.

A mechanism is needed to handle possible resentments.

Head count can be adjusted by early retirement.

Conditions of service may be aligned if institutions are of similar origins. If different, consider pension arrangements, salary scales, titles, contracts.

Identifying roles where no appropriate place:

- will be influenced by availability of funds, age of staff, urgency of rationalisation.

Unions

Unions will be involved in the removal of staff and their counselling. They will also push for disturbance allowances, particularly if there is geographical distance involved and will aim to protect employees.

Finance

There may well need to be pump priming to enhance capabilities in certain areas.

There may need to be new cross-subsidies arranged, or a new strategic fund.

Sorting out payroll arrangements is critical for the maintenance of employee morale and for not sending the wrong messages.

External stakeholders

If there is media interest:

- control the process
- monitor what is being said
- maintain a united front
- ensure representation from both sides
- co-ordinate press releases
- ensure clear message
- emphasise positive local implications
- emphasise positive image and mission.

Local authority:

- maintain good relations especially if planning permissions required or closures intended.

Source: Derived from Palfreyman, Thomas and Warner (1998). Published by kind permission of the authors from 'How to manage a merger . . . or avoid one', Heist Marketing Services for Universities and Colleges

Lessons from higher education mergers

Temple and Whitchurch (1994) examined a significant number of mergers between parts of London University.[3]

Lessons from these mergers include:

1 Central administration and task force planning initiatives can encourage change alongside pump-priming funding and a support structure for addressing external and internal resource considerations.

2 The combination of two or more weak departments does not make a stronger, less vulnerable one. Greater restructuring will be needed.

3 Academic and physical restructuring requires long-term investments. Results will not be immediate and this will probably affect student and staff morale.

4 Difficult decisions over resource and staffing issues will be encountered and are unlikely to please all.

CHAPTER 6: SUMMARY

- The NFP sector presents a particular set of difficulties regarding mergers.

- Stakeholders are many and varied with often conflicting agendas.

- NFPs will prefer to remain distinct in enacting their particular set of core beliefs.

- Significant external pressures have generally been necessary to overcome the 'singularity' of NFPs.

- The rise of a more managerial approach to NFPs is resulting in greater institutional merger initiatives.

- The involvement of employees in merger negotiations often leads to breakdown, so their role is being de-emphasised.

- Employees cannot be divorced from the 'service' and are critical for success where integration is intended.

Notes

1   A letter from the Deaconess anaesthesiologists protests an orderly departure (*The Wall Street Journal*, 10 June 1999).

2   The rise of many distance learning and electronically based modes of delivery may radically affect the importance of physical proximity.

3   The medical school in 1983 (St Thomas's, Guy's, Royal Dental Hospital to form the United Medical and Dental School), a new King's College 1985 (Chelsea, Queen Elizabeth and King's Colleges), Royal Holloway and Bedford New College 1985 (Bedford and Royal Holloway Colleges), City and East London Confederation 1988 (The London and St Bartholomew's Hospital Medical Colleges, and Queen Mary College), Queen Mary and Westfield College 1989 (Queen Mary and Westfield Colleges).

Postscript

Mergers and acquisitions have a major impact upon the structure of business and executive lives. Estimates suggest that one in five executives will have direct experience of an acquisition during their working lives. This leads to high levels of interest in the topic and many rumours of their effects to circulate.

This book has shown that care needs to be taken when attempting to generalise from such stories, as acquisitions come in all shapes and sizes. For instance, a common error is for executives, highly experienced in asset purchases, to believe that more complex purchases can be integrated with such ease. A common fear of acquired staff is that there will be blood letting, although if they represent a valuable set of capabilities the acquirer will be much more likely to worry about how to keep them. With acquisitions ranging enormously in size, scope, configuration and complexity, any 'golden rules' are likely to be hard pressed to have equal value. However, many practitioner sources do suggest 'golden rules' for post-acquisition success. This report shows that some of those recommendations, which have crept into common acquisition parlance, are dangerously misleading. The following table gives examples against which are important qualifications stemming from the text of this report.

Table P.1　Some 'golden rules' for post-acquisition success

Often cited rules	Qualification
If the acquisition strategy is good, then the acquisition will succeed	This assumes that pre-acquisition planning is directly linked to performance and overlooks post-acquisition integration as the creator or destroyer of value.
Speed is vital	In taking charge of the acquisition, this is true. However, in making substantial changes, this depends entirely upon the appropriate acquisition style.
Acquirer should impose decisions – 'the conquering heroes'	This may be applicable in subjugation and isolation acquisitions, but would be damaging in other circumstances.
Involve acquired employees in decisions	This is applicable in collaborative acquisitions, but would seriously delay other acquisition styles.
Focus on getting value out	Whilst the sentiment of focusing upon the value drivers may be laudable, this often becomes a case of 'cost outing' which, whilst appropriate in some circumstances, can act against the spirit and purpose of the acquisition.

Often cited rules	Qualification
'Communicate, communicate, communicate'	This is often interpreted as 'volume' of top down communication from day one. However, it is not so simple. Communication is vital but volume up front is not enough. It cannot be content-free, it has to be honest, requires multiple channels and must be continuous. The level of dialogue should reflect the post-acquisition style.

Some of the 'golden rules' are therefore, perhaps, not so golden. However, we suggest that some may continue to provide useful pointers for executives perceiving acquisitions to embody significant variety and complexity.

Pre-deal*

Relationship:	If possible, establish a good pre-deal relationship.
Responsibility:	Appoint an overall acquisition manager who has significant clout within both companies.
Continuity:	Ensure that the acquisition manager or steering group is fully involved before the deal and throughout the integration process.
Clear vision:	Have a clear idea of the purpose and direction of the acquired company and also its implications for the acquirer.
Good management:	Ensure the acquired company has or will have a good management team.
Detailed post-acquisition planning:	Ensure that this process is well under way prior to taking charge and make use of any pre-closing window.

Post-deal

1. **Actively take charge:**	Clear leadership and vision are essential for stabilising the acquisitions. Re-engage employees, set expectations and gain support of other stakeholders. Show that the world has changed and avoid a post-acquisition vacuum at all costs.

---

* This book does not focus on pre-acquisition considerations and so this list is from a post-acquisition perspective.

(This doesn't mean that the rest of the integration has to be rushed.)

2. **Communicate:**

Instantly Use multilevel communications immediately upon ownership to inform acquired employees of the spirit and purpose of the acquisition, and set expectations.

Honestly Recognise that an acquisition is as much a psychological contract as a legal one. Ensure messages show high integrity so that an atmosphere of trust is established.

Deeply Ensure clear, formal communications links to inform employees of the progress of the integration.

Work at informal channels for effective dissemination and receiving of general attitudes and feelings.

Continuously This is critical for managing expectations in a rapidly changing environment.

Interactively Give employees the opportunity to raise their concerns rather than let their fears and the rumour mill get out of control.

3. **Evaluate business and controls:** Find out what really has been purchased and adjust plans. Get the acquired company's accounts expressed in the acquirer's terms (but do not be too zealous in detailed requirements at the outset).

4. **Establish mutual cultural awareness:** To avoid the worst problems of culture clash and to establish the foundations of change.

5. **Manage the politics:** Acquiring managers can use 'the conquering hero' syndrome to further their own ambitions. Acquired managers may say 'the horse can talk'.

6. **Show commitment:** Where possible, show actual commitment rather than just words. Even small actions have a substantial impact.

7. **Keep your eyes on the commercial football:** Don't let the complexities of post-acquisition management cause you to ignore your competitive standing (particularly as competitors will re-double efforts to win market share at this time).

8. **Value differences:** In the rush to reduce costs through standardisation, remember that it is the differences which will add value in the medium term if handled sensitively.

9. **Value tacit knowledge:** Do not underestimate the importance of knowledge which is not written down. People's collective heads may be more valuable than paper based information.

10. **Follow a consistent approach to integration:** Different post-acquisition styles present different managerial challenges and result in different benefits. Consistency of approach is important for success.

There are several ways in which acquisitions can be managed. Questions, such as 'should we wield an axe or a scalpel?' and 'should we act like Ghengis Khan or Ghandi?', can be aligned with the way in which value is to be achieved from the acquisition and the level of tension between organisational fit and strategic fit. Higher rewards are generally linked with greater complexity and risk, so acquirers should reflect upon their strategic horizons, their embedded acquisition experience and their learning capacity.

In the words of one CEO, *'It will always cost you more than you expect, and take longer than you think'*.

TWELVE TIPS ON BEST PRACTICE

Post-acquisition management is a hands-on process with high risks and substantial rewards. There are no golden rules to guarantee success but all these things will help:

- Provide obvious leadership and vision
- Meet and talk to employees frequently
- Maintain effective communications internally and externally
- Respond quickly to setbacks
- Provide time to test ideas and recommendations
- Select the right people for the right jobs
- Trust your instincts when judging people
- Maintain your sights on the big picture
- Create a culture of success
- Watch how competitors are reacting to your changes
- Be prepared to change initial plans
- Reward innovation and results
- Insist on adherence to management controls and agreed budgets
- Exercise loose/tight controls on operational managers.

A senior manager's working checklist for practical implementation

However many management books you have bought, however frequently you read the *Wall Street Journal* or *Harvard Business Review*, there comes a time when you are on your own. Responsibilities have been allocated, expectations raised and it is time to deliver.

Acquisitions demand clear action, informed thinking, determination and courage. To help practising managers to interpret and convert material in this book into practical working documents for their own use, this section draws upon the experience of Collinson Grant Consultants who have spent 25 years assisting managers in restructuring and improving the performance of large businesses. This section draws upon their experience in the form of a series of working checklists.

The checklists are modelled on a **subjugation** style of acquisition, although all the techniques and tasks can be applied to other acquisition styles with suitable adjustments for intensity and timing. The checklists are designed to supplement acquirers' internal expertise and 'standard' approaches as well as stimulate thought. They focus upon:

1 *Interpreting the background* to the acquisition – why you are where you are and knowing where you want to get to.

2 *Understanding the process* of managing a newly acquired business.

3 *Defining the specific managerial tasks* that need to be completed to secure improvements.

4 *Setting out best practice* in managing the post-acquisition process.

5 *Analysing risks and unexpected events* and how to respond to them.

GETTING STARTED

Setting the scene: internally

A sound framework for judging success is essential. This needs to provide, as far as possible, objective, quantified measures of what is planned and when it should be achieved. The main 'drivers for change' need to be identified and then amplified into specific improvement tasks with measurable targets.

Checklist 1 Assessing priorities and criteria for measuring success

Drivers for change	Priority High/Low/ N/A	Improvement tasks	Measurement criteria	Time frame
Establish a presence in a new market				
Increase market share				
Gain new brands				
Extend product range or services				
Access distribution channels				
Acquire new technology				
Gain new skills/know-how				
Build reputation				
Gain additional manufacturing capacity				
Reduce production/distribution costs				
Reduce central overheads				
Exploit synergies between business units				
Take out competitor(s)				
Reduce risks from environmental lobby				
Reduce exposure to new legislation				
Others				

Note: This list is by no means exhaustive

As all seasoned acquirers know, the companies may have been needing major restructuring for some time and the act of acquisition provides a golden opportunity. Drivers for change then may not just be limited to the specific act of acquisition but may be broader in nature. The important issue is that there is coherence to the restructuring rather than a piecemeal approach, which may result in more harm than good.

Setting the scene: externally

Successful managers are only too aware that 'perception is reality'. In the very public arena of a multi-million pound acquisition, whatever managers do and what they achieve, the perceptions of others are what really count. The crucial voyeurs are customers, investors, media and employees – lose the confidence of any of these groups, at any time, and the odds on achieving real gains are reduced dramatically. Yet there is much that can be done at the outset to reduce this risk: in particular, managing all stakeholders' expectations:

- at the outset; and

- dynamically throughout the process.

For outside stakeholders, the principal criteria in judging your performance are by reference to your declared objectives. Senior executives have only themselves to blame if their initial announcements or projections are overly ambitious or just downright unrealistic.

Checklist 2 Where am I starting from?

Review, understand and analyse:

- Who is watching me?

- What does each one of them expect and when?

- Who are the most important players?

- What is the medium- and longer-term strategy for the new acquisition?

  - Where do I want the business to be: in one and three years' time?

- What are the implications for the whole business?

- What are the key facts that I should check?

- How will my particular skills and experience be helpful?

- What are the gaps in my skills and knowledge?

- What help and resources are likely to be available:

  - in the parent group?

  - in the acquired company?

  - from external advisers and consultants?

- What are the risks to me and how should I reduce them?

- Who might be my best ally?

- Who might stab me in the back?

- Whose advice can I trust and whose must I treat with caution?

MANAGING A NEWLY ACQUIRED BUSINESS

Managing a newly acquired business means more demanding time scales, more intense stress and greater uncertainty. However, the cycle of continuous action remains a useful overview.

Fig. A.1 Cycle of continuous action

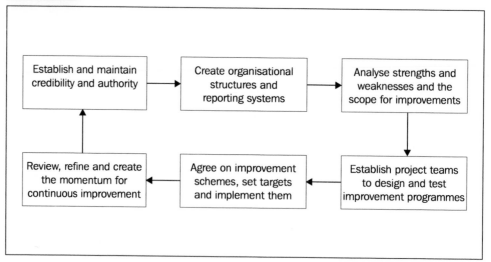

This basic structure needs to be coupled with specific actions relating to taking charge of the acquisition:

- taking physical, legal and *moral* control of the new company

- sustaining the performance and image of the business under the glare of external observers

- responding quickly to previously unknown weaknesses in the acquired business

- ensuring that the business can operate satisfactorily within the overall strategy of its new owners

- achieving early results that build the confidence to secure more fundamental long-term changes.

The new chief executive has to be able to demonstrate quickly the ability to deliver measurable benefits. Whatever the circumstances of the acquisition – however quickly it took place, however big the premium paid, however much publicity it attracted – there are a number of key tasks to be completed within the first two to three months.

Checklist 3 Eight tasks to secure managerial control

Task	Elements
1 Obtain physical and managerial control	- establish cash and bank controls - ensure legal framework for action - confirm financial balances - install expenditure controls on capital and revenue - improve debtor controls - establish/improve inventory controls - confirm tax, national insurance and VAT liabilities

Task	Elements
2 Assess senior managers	■ assess finance director and remove if necessary ■ determine options for new FD, financial controller or interim executive ■ assess key operational managers by performance in early project tasks ■ consider use of psychometric testing and assessment centres ■ review options for transferring managers from parent company, permanently or on loan
3 Manage the communications strategy	■ take personal responsibility for communications ■ ensure consistent, simple, accurate and timely messages ■ meet managers quickly ■ communicate effectively with employees and meet as many as possible ■ consider organising a management conference ■ obtain candid comment on delivery/content and respond accordingly ■ use formal and informal channels
4 Secure the business's current performance	■ clarify profit forecast for the current year and ensure it is realised ■ take immediate actions as required: – confirm/review contracts, arrangements, prices and terms with key suppliers/customers – secure key staff with retention bonuses/contracts – reduce costs – delay or speed up investments – others?
5 Introduce corporate financial controls and reporting systems	■ transfer common financial controls ■ establish consistent reporting systems for assessing performance internally and throughout the group ■ determine immediate strengths and weaknesses of information technology resources ■ consider likely major organisational changes and their implication for organisational structure and appropriate controls/systems

Task	Elements
6 Evaluate the state of the business	■ organisational accountabilities ■ managerial and operational controls ■ financial analyses and operating ratios ■ major products/services and contribution ■ information systems ■ promotion and selling ■ purchasing and supply ■ pay and reward systems ■ conditions of employment ■ responsiveness to change: people and systems
7 Select broad targets for improvement Identify Critical Success Factors (CSFs) by testing sensitivity of profits to changes in specific activities	■ market share, new markets/products ■ cost reductions – labour, materials, services ■ improved margins and profitability ■ better cashflows ■ more efficient use of the supply chain ■ enhanced use of technologies ■ improved business processes: manufacturing, services or support functions
8 Demonstrate commitment/vision/ leadership	■ visible, early and decisive actions ■ focus on achievable quick gains ■ openness in communications ■ provide scope for individual managerial action ■ reward results and endeavour

Success in each of the eight steps will indicate to internal and external observers that the business is being *managed*, that it has a clear *direction*, and that a *strategy* for further improvement is being evolved.

This is the essential primary stage to be completed properly before the full process for implementing radical change can be introduced. It also assumes that sufficient care has been taken in planning the integration before the deal is signed and essential prerequisites completed.

A PROCESS FOR ACHIEVING CHANGE

An overview of the processes for securing managerial control and implementing radical change is shown in Figure A.2.

Action is undertaken under the careful scrutiny of customers, competitors, investors, employees and suppliers. The five stages of implementation each have their own sub-components and are supported by agile communications and robust project management. A tough and trusted project manager/chaser who will not accept excuses for delays or failures is an invaluable ally.

Fig. A.2 Process for securing managerial control and implementing radical change

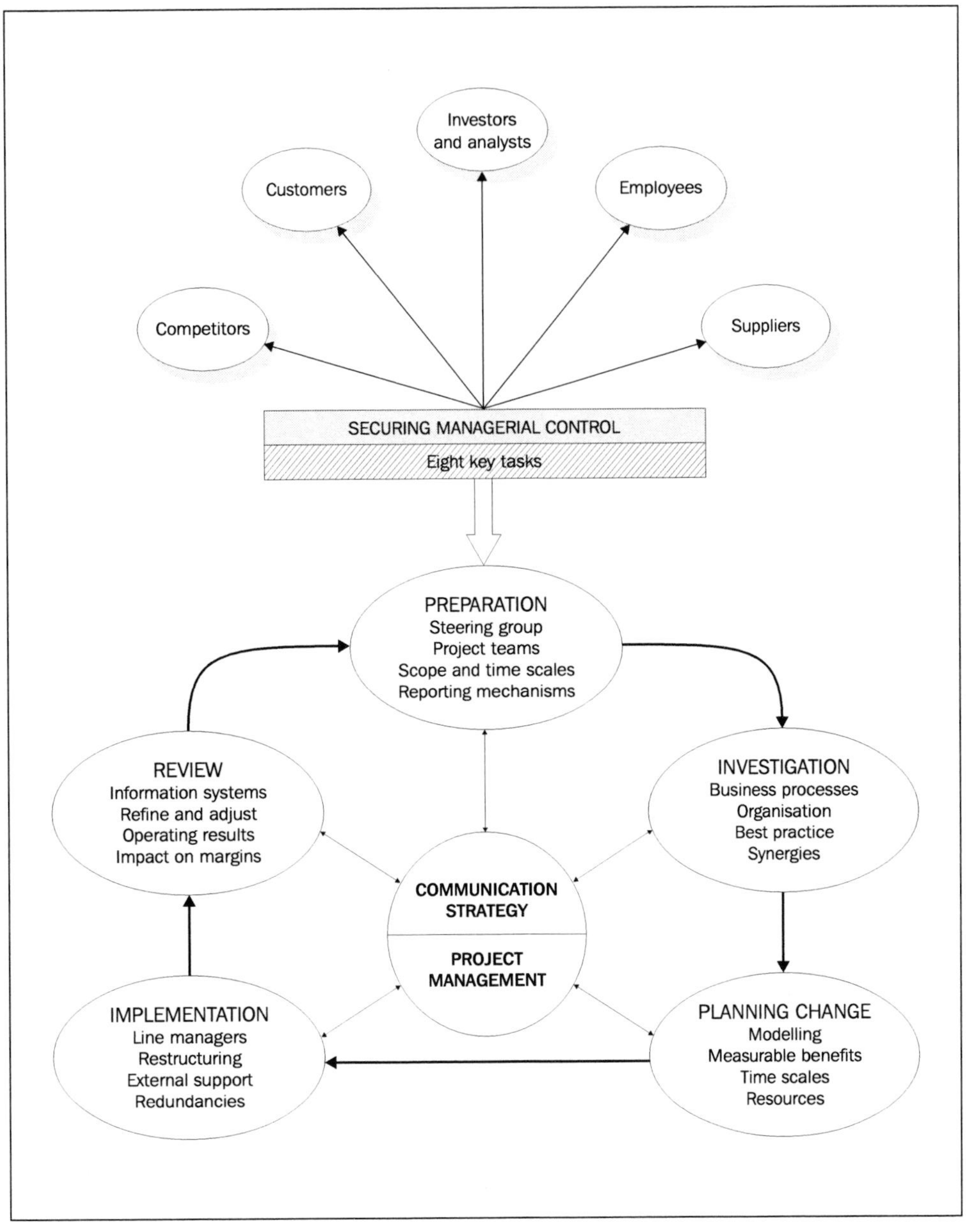

Preparation

A lot can be done in the pre-acquisition phase to prepare and plan for the implementation process. These activities will build upon the core values and disciplines of the acquirer's business. To oversee this critical process, an overall steering group should be established, supported by a number of project teams. The steering group will include most (if not all) of the senior executives in the company. In many cases it is useful to include a representative from the human resources department.

Checklist 4 Steering group questions

- Who has ultimate managerial responsibility?

- Who is in the steering group, how often does it meet and what are its functions?

- What project teams are to be established, and which combination of line managers, internal and transferred specialists and external advisers will they use?

- What tasks will be set for the project teams and how well defined will they be?

- What time scales are appropriate for the tasks set?

- How is progress to be reported: from project teams to the steering group, between project teams, to the main board, to employees and to others?

- How will the steering group contribute to and maintain a grip on the day-to-day running of the business?

Investigation and analysis

No matter how thorough the pre-acquisition analysis, there is often a gap between expectation and reality. The early evaluation of the business will reveal a number of immediate tasks for action and the broad targets for improvements will define the other priorities for early investigation. It is important that care is taken to set up project teams, with clear objectives and tasks that are achievable in the time allotted.

Checklist 5 Tasks for project teams

- Analyse current business performance

- Define operational strengths and weaknesses

- Compare and contrast working methods throughout the business(es)

- Identify synergies

- Discover good practice.

Typically, in the early stages project teams will use common analytical tools such as tally charts, fishbone diagrams, Pareto analysis and process mapping, as well as more complex methods. Sometimes it is useful to establish smaller working groups with specific, short-term targets for investigating problems and generating or testing data. The process of creating and operating project teams is a useful learning experience for the business, provides opportunities for developing staff, building cohesion amongst employees and sustaining improvements in the future.

At the end of the investigations, project teams should be in a position to report back to the steering group with a concise summary of deliverables.

Checklist 6 Project team deliverables

- What has been investigated?
- How has it been investigated (method used)?
- What are the essential characteristics of the business unit or process under review?
- What are its operational strengths and weaknesses?
- What improvements or changes are possible and recommended?
- What benefits are likely to accrue?
- How quickly can the benefits be achieved?

Planning the changes

Determining which improvement projects to implement and when is a critical step. There is still an imperative to secure easily recognisable and significant early benefits, but at this stage a more systematic decision-making mechanism is called for. The chief executive should by now be getting a better feel for the new business, be able to understand its subtleties and underlying culture and be ready and able to put flesh on the bones of the provisional improvement strategy. The selection of initiatives to introduce substantial change and their phasing will have an important influence on the medium- and longer-term outcomes of the acquisition.

A formal assessment by the steering group of each proposed improvement plan is recommended. Some will fit into an obvious hierarchy for scheduling, others will be essentially stand-alone projects. Whilst the following checklist is just a starting point for a more sophisticated process, it is helpful to ask the following questions for each project under consideration.

Checklist 7 Assessment and approval of improvement projects

- How is the project defined: scope, location etc.?
- What are the specific, predicted benefits?
- How do these contribute to the overall strategy?
- What will the financial cost be in revenue and capital expenditure?
- How soon will the benefits be realised?
- What does success depend upon?
- Can a financial model of the proposed solution be constructed with 'what if' scenarios?
- What managerial and other staff resources will be needed?
- What will be the impact on current operations?
- What external help will be needed?

- Does the project overlap with/contribute to other initiatives?
- Are there opportunities for introducing best practice or benchmarking?
- What are the risks of proceeding?
- Has a credible project plan been constructed?

Implementation

Major organisational changes demand the commitment of the whole steering group as well as a dedicated, multi-disciplinary project team. Line managers should be involved at every stage and will normally take the lead for discrete improvement projects. This is essential to reinforce their ownership of the project and commitment to achieving results. Internal specialists and external consultants have a part to play, but in a supporting rather than a leading role.

Once approval has been given for an initiative to proceed, actions should take place quickly according to the previously agreed project plan. Many managers are now familiar with formal project planning and control techniques supported by appropriate software, such as Microsoft Project, Prince 2, Opera and Project Scheduler. This systematic approach should be encouraged.

Checklist 8   Implementing change

- Are line managers committed to the project and do they fully understand their responsibilities?
- Have managerial accountabilities been set out clearly, including budgetary constraints?
- How is a vision of future activities being developed and communicated?
- Are new managerial reporting systems being used to their full advantage?
- How are employees being motivated to maintain commitment and enthusiasm for the project?
- How is progress being reported and are variances from the plan being identified and responded to?
- Is it necessary to facilitate change with transitional working arrangements?
- Are there any opportunities to make progress more quickly than predicted and should they be taken?
- How are unexpected difficulties being managed and are they likely to affect the eventual outcome?
- Are opportunities being taken to publicise early successes?
- Are there any important lessons to be learnt for the Group or other subsidiaries?
- How will the benefits be consolidated and sustained in the longer term?

Reviewing progress

Reviewing progress routinely and on an ad hoc basis is the final stage of the cycle. Comparison of results against forecasts provides the stimulus for additional actions, adjustment of targets or provision of extra resources. This leads cyclically to a continuous process of review and refinement.

A 'reporting' discipline should be established within the project teams and to the steering group. This group must maintain an overview of the performance of the whole business and how it is being affected by each of the improvement projects (as well as other contemporaneous external events). Whenever possible, reports should be made using the newly installed management information and reporting systems. This has the additional benefit of reinforcing their use, testing their effectiveness and providing a consistent framework for reporting across the business.

Checklist 9   **Steering group review questions**

- Which projects are on schedule and which are not?

- Where are additional resources likely to be needed?

- Are any of the projects experiencing unforeseen outcomes, either positive or negative?

- How committed are line managers to the project, their new tasks and responsibilities?

- Have any new ideas been generated?

- Which new ideas should be promulgated throughout the business?

- Which project plans need to be adjusted and how quickly?

- How should employees, investors, customers and others be informed of progress?

- What is the overall impact of the implementation on the business's operational performance?

IMPROVEMENT INITIATIVES

Integrating an acquisition and achieving real improvement in its performance are complex tasks. They require a carefully co-ordinated combination of strategic, tactical and operational activities. The preceding sections have illustrated how this process is initiated and managed; here we describe the options for different improvement initiatives and how they overlap and reinforce each other.

Change can take place on three broad fronts:

- major restructuring and organisational design;
- company-wide improvement initiatives that affect all or most of the business;
- specific, department-focused projects for enhanced performance.

The following checklist sets out the main categories of improvement schemes and indicates their content and the implications for the business.

Checklist 10 **Categories and characteristics of improvement initiatives**

	Improvement initiative	Scope and actions
S T R A T E G I C	Organisational restructuring (business unit)	*Scope* ■ functions of principal business units ■ key business processes ■ managerial accountabilities ■ financial and operational controls ■ outsourcing manufacturing/services ■ shared services *Actions* ■ integrate structure with strategy ■ assess/replace senior managers ■ analyse processes and activities ■ rationalise operations across the group ■ develop financial models ■ introduce redundancy/re-deployment programmes ■ sell surplus business sites ■ audit information technology resources ■ define the new interface with other departments ■ benchmark internally/externally
S T R A T E G I C / T A C T I C A L	Culture, policy and systems (company-wide)	*Scope* ■ human resources (development) strategy ■ management information systems ■ culture for sustaining improvements ■ employee relations ■ communication ■ quality and customer service *Actions* ■ restructure pay and benefits to reinforce strategic goals ■ harmonise terms and conditions of employment ■ clarify short-term and long-term goals ■ reward managerial and individual attainments ■ implement best practice ■ survey employee opinions and attitudes (one-off and regularly)

Improvement initiative	Scope and actions
TACTICAL Performance improvement projects (department-based)	*Scope* ■ productivity schemes ■ supply chain process ■ self-managed teams ■ activity based costing ■ cycle-time reduction ■ optimum design for products and systems ■ customer service measures and performance ■ maintenance schemes ■ total quality management *Actions* ■ use management reporting that prompts action ■ introduce continuous improvement teams ■ process mapping ■ rated activity sampling ■ activity based costing ■ process activity analysis ■ encourage managerial autonomy ■ benchmark against business excellence models and competitors ■ define service level agreements ■ take early action and maintain it by continuous refinement
TACTICAL Cost reductions (company-wide and department)	*Scope* ■ direct labour costs ■ purchasing services and materials ■ management awareness and culture ■ inventory controls ■ working capital ■ property portfolio ■ rationalise surplus plant capacity ■ unification/consolidation of manufacturing and processing capabilities *Actions* ■ audit and take action on overheads ■ make one-off and annualised savings ■ restructure debts ■ tighten financial reporting systems ■ cut manpower and overtime ■ consolidate suppliers

	Improvement initiative	Scope and actions

S
T
R
A
T
E
G
I
C
/
T
A
C
T
I
C
A
L
	Market driven
	(company-wide and department)
		Scope
		■ new product/market focus
		   – product analysis and rationalisation
		   – product development and launch
		■ routes to the market
		■ customer relationship management
		■ pricing review and strategy
		■ selling processes
		■ tactics and strategy for longer-term market promotion planning
		
		Actions
		■ survey customers
		■ audit marketing, pricing and promotion
		■ analyse competitors' current actions and future strategy
		■ analyse and manage the database
		■ audit the profitability of products
		■ research and market planning

IMPLEMENTATION DIFFICULTIES AND GETTING BACK ON TRACK

Leading organisational change and securing tangible benefits is hard work. It is easy to become distracted, especially if you still have the responsibility of managing the business. When things start to go wrong, the symptoms are often all too familiar:

■ tasks take more time than expected

■ unexpected problems arise

■ competing activities distract attention

■ restructuring costs increase sharply

■ skills, abilities and leadership are inadequate

■ insufficient attention is given to detail

■ inadequate training and support are available for new processes

■ external factors affect progress adversely

■ the implementation programme is neither defined nor monitored carefully.

Rather than blaming everything in sight and becoming submerged by a myriad of difficulties in fire-fighting, the remedies for getting back on track lie in taking a step back, drawing on your managerial experience and realising that success is critically dependent on the motivation and performance of people. Having a team that you can trust (with specific responsibilities) is an important prerequisite for achieving results. It is essential to have confidence in the managers who will have to implement innovation and take unpopular decisions. Managers operating new processes should be given precise and tightly monitored targets for performance, together with the autonomy to devise the tactics for achieving them.

It is almost certain that some of the incumbents will not be up to the task. They should be replaced swiftly and painlessly, resisting the claims that individuals have indispensable skills or knowledge. The considerations when deciding how to remove directors and senior managers include:

- Are they shareholders?
- What legal constraints are there to terminating the contract?
- What key knowledge or skills do they have?
- What key relationships do they have with customers or others?
- Can they be transferred elsewhere in the business or must they go?
- How much will it cost?

Despite the best planning, the latest technology and a fully committed board of directors, success comes down largely to the energy, enthusiasm and skills of line managers – 'the marzipan layer'. They must be given room to operate – **act, innovate and test** – but also be disciplined enough to act within a formal control and reporting system. A framework of *loose–tight* controls helps to motivate action, stimulate ambition and reward endeavour while at the same time retaining essential **command and control**. This careful balance in managing managers is *the* critical success factor.

Table A.1	Getting it right
STRATEGY	Translated into **specific managerial tasks**
COMMUNICATION	Ensure it is **two-way**
PLANNING	In appropriate **detail**
COMMITMENT	From managers **and** employees
RESOURCES	**Sufficient** internal **time** allocated and nominated external resources
LEADERSHIP	A nominated **champion** for success
TARGETS	Realistic and **time-bound**
PROGRESS	Measured **regularly** and **published**

Bibliography

Consultancy references

AMR	See Rankine
Ernst and Young	See Angwin/Ernst and Young
Collinson Grant	
Coopers and Lybrand	
A.T. Kearney	
KPMG	
London Consultancy	
McKinsey	See Chapman *et al.*
Mercer Consultancy	
PricewaterhouseCoopers	See Feldman and Spratt

Angwin, D. N. (1995a) 'Taking charge of a newly acquired company', *ESRC Conference*. Vancouver, Canada. Working Paper

Angwin, D. N. (1995b) 'The dynamics of post-acquisition management', *British Academy of Management*. Sheffield. Working Paper

Angwin, D. N. (1996a) 'After the fall', *Management Today*, February

Angwin, D. N. (1996b) 'The dynamics of post-acquisition management', *Warwick Business School Research Paper*, 204, January

Angwin, D. N. (1997) 'Insiders, outsiders, top management teams and post-acquisition change', *British Academy of Management*. London. Refereed Paper

Angwin, D. N. (1998a) 'Should managing executives stay or go after acquisition? The case for using insiders or outsiders', *Strategic Management Society Conference*. Orlando, USA

Angwin, D. N. (1998b) 'Post-acquisition management of corporate take-overs in the United Kingdom', PhD thesis, Warwick University

Angwin, D. N. and Ernst and Young (1996) *European Acquisitions: Getting it Right*. Ernst and Young/Warwick Business School

Angwin, D. N. and Ernst and Young (1997) *The First 90 Days*. Ernst and Young/Warwick Business School

Angwin, D. N. and Savill, B. (1997) 'Strategic perspectives on European cross-border acquisitions: a view from top European executives', *European Management Journal*, 15, 4, August

Angwin, D. N. and Wensley, R. (1997) 'The acquisition challenge', hot topics, *Warwick Business School Briefing Paper*, 1, 4

Angwin, D. N., Wensley, R. and Ernst and Young (1995) *Key Success Factors in Acquisition Management*. Ernst and Young/Warwick Business School

Anslinger, P. L. and Copeland, T. E. (1996) 'Growth through acquisitions: a fresh look', *Harvard Business Review*, January–February

Arkansas, R. N., de Monaco, C. J. and Francis, S. C. (1998) 'Making the deal real: how, GE capital integrates acquisitions', *Harvard Business Review*, January–February: 165–78

Ball, M. (1988) 'For better for worse. Merger partners discuss blending systems, style', *Computerworld*, 22, 12–16, cited in Merali, Y. and McKiernan, P. (1993) 'The strategic positioning of information systems in post acquisition management', *Journal of Strategic Information Systems*

Bauman, R. P., Jackson, P. and Lawrence, J. T. (1997) *From Promise to Performance: A Journey of Transformation at SmithKline Beecham*. Harvard Business School Press

Beatty, R. P. and Zajac, E. J. (1987) 'CEO change and firm performance in large corporations: succession effects', *Strategic Management Journal*, 8: 305–17

Bleeke, J. and Ernst, D. (1993) *Collaborating to Compete: Using Strategic Alliances and Acquisitions in the Global Marketplace*, Willey

Buono, A. F. and Bowditch, J. L. (1989) *The Human Side of Mergers and Acquisitions: Managing Collisions Between People and Organisations*. San Francisco: Jossey–Bass

Business International (1992) 'Making acquisitions work', The Economist Group, Report M184

Calori, R. and Lubatkin, M. (1994) 'Euro Mergers 1993: Viewpoints and predictions', in Krogh, G. v., Sinatra, A. and Singh, H. (1994) *The Management of Corporate Acquisitions*. Macmillan Press Ltd

Carlyle, R. E. (1986) 'Mergers: a raw deal for MIS', *Datamation*, September 15

Cartwright, S. and Cooper, C. (1992 and 1996) *Acquisitions – The Human Factor*. Butterworth/Heinemann

Chapman, T. L., Dempsey, J. J., Ramsdell, G. and Bell, T. E. (1998) 'Purchasing's big moment – after a merger', *The McKinsey Quarterly*, 1: 57–56

Chatterjee, S. (1986) 'Types of synergy and economic value: the impact of acquisitions on merging and rival firms', *Strategic Management Journal*, 7: 119–139

Coopers and Lybrand (1992) *A Review of the Acquisitions Experience of Major UK Companies*. Coopers and Lybrand

Coopers and Lybrand (1996) *Speed Makes the Difference: A Survey of Mergers and Acquisitions*. Coopers and Lybrand

Drucker, P. F. (1993) *Post Capitalist Society*, Butterworth/Heinemann

Durman, P. (1998) 'Leschly blames Glaxo for failed merger', *The Times*, 23 April

Empson, L. (1999) 'Phoney wars and high school dances: the evolving process of integration in mergers between professional service firms', *Academy of Management Conference*. Paper

Feldman, M. and Spratt, M. F. (1999) *Five Frogs on a Log: A CEO's Field Guide to Accelerating the Transition in Mergers, Acquisitions and Gut Wrenching Change*. PricewaterhouseCoopers/Harper Business

Franks, J. and Mayer, C. (1996) 'Hostile take-overs and the correction of managerial failure', *Journal of Financial Economics*, 40: 163–181

Gouillart, F. J. and Kelly, J. N. (1995) *Transforming the Organisation*. McGraw-Hill

Grinyer, P. and Spender, J-C. (1979) *Turnaround: Managerial Recipes for Strategic Success*. London. Associated Business Press

Hambrick, D. C. and Cannella, Jnr. A. A. (1993) 'Relative standing: a framework for understanding departures of acquired executives', *Academy of Management Journal*, 36: 733–62

Haspeslagh, P. C. and Farquhar, A. B. (1994) 'The acquisition integration process: a contingent framework', in Krogh, von G., Sinatra, A. and Singh, H. (eds) (1994) *The Management of Corporate Acquisitions*. Macmillan Press Ltd

Haspeslagh P. C. and Jemison (1991) *Managing Acquisitions*, The Free Press

Hayes, R. H. (1979) 'The human side of acquisitions', *Management Review*, 68: 41–6

Hayward, M. (1999) 'Acquiror learning from acquisition experience: evidence from 1985–95', *Academy Management Proceedings*, Chicago

Hofstede, G. (1993) 'Cultural constraints in management theories', *Academy of Management Executive*, 7, 1

Hsiao, R. (1998) 'Dynamics of knowledge transfer: a discovery-oriented framework', *Strategic Management Society Conference*. Orlando, USA

Hsieh, T.-Y. and Bear, S. (1996) 'The first 100 days' *Management Decision*, September, 34(5) 30–32

Hubbard, N. (1999) *Acquisition: Strategy and Implementation*, Macmillan Business

Hunt, J. (1990) 'Changing pattern of acquisition behaviour in take-overs and consequences for acquisition processes', *Strategic Management Journal*, 11: 66–77

Hunt, J., Lees, S., Grumbar, J. J. and Vivian, P. D. (1986) *Acquisitions – The Human Factor*. London Business School/Egon Zehnder International

Jemison, D. B. and Sitkin, S. B. (1986) 'Acquisition: The process can be the problem', *Harvard Business Review*, March–April

Johnson, G. and Scholes, K. (1999) *Exploring Corporate Strategy*. 5th edn. Prentice Hall Europe

Jones, C. S. (1985a) 'An empirical study of the role of management accounting systems following take-over or merger', *Accounting, Organisations and Society*, 10, 2: 177–200

Jones, C. S. (1985b) 'An empirical study of the evidence for contingency theories of management accounting systems in conditions of rapid change', *Accounting, Organisations and Society*, 10, 3: 303–328

Junius, K. (1997) 'Economies of scale: a survey of the empirical literature', Kiel Institute of World Economics. Economics Working Paper 813, May

Kaplan, R. S. and Norton, D. P. (1992) 'The balanced scorecard – measures that drive performance', *Harvard Business Review*, January–February

Kesner and Fowler (1997) 'When consultants and clients clash', *Harvard Business Review*, November–December

Kitching, J. (1974) 'Winning and losing with European acquisitions', *Harvard Business Review*, March–April

KPMG (1998) 'Deal watch' – The KPMG Corporate Finance 1998 Survey, KPMG

Krishnan, H. A. Miller, A. and Judge, W. Q. (1997) 'Diversification and TMT complimentarity: is performance and improved merging similar or dissimilar teams', *Strategic Management Journal*, 18, 5: 361–74

Krogh, G. v., Sinatra, A. and Singh, H. (1994) *The Management of Corporate Acquisitions*. Macmillan Press Ltd

Kusewitt, J. B. Jr (1985) 'An exploratory study of strategic acquisition factors relating to performance', *Strategic Management Journal*, 16

Lengel, R. H. and Daft, R. L. (1988) 'The selection of communication media as an executive skill', *The Academy of Management Excutive*, 11(3) 225–32

London Consulting (1998) *The Use of Teams in Post-Acquisition Management*, London Consulting

Lubatkin, M. (1983) 'Mergers and the performance of the acquiring firm', *Academy of Management Review*, 8, 2: 218–225

McCann, J. E. and Gilkey, R. (1988) *Creating and Managing Successful Mergers and Acquisitions*. Englewood Cliffs NJ: Prentice Hall

McKiernan, P. and Merali, Y. (1995) 'Integrating information systems after a merger', *Long Range Planning*: 54–62

Merali, Y. and McKieman, P. (1993) 'The strategic positioning of information systems in post-acquisition management', *Journal of Strategic Information Systems*, 2, June 2

Mercer Management Consultancy (1995) *Mercer Management Journal*, Mercer Management Consulting

Mirvis, P. H. and Marks, M. L. (1992) *Managing the Merger: Making It Work*, Prentice Hall

Nahavandi, A. and Malekzadeh, A. R. (1988) 'Acculturation in mergers and acquisitions', *Academy of Management Review*, 13, 1: 79–90

Palfreyman, D., Thomas, H. and Warner, D. (1998) How To Manage a Merger... or Avoid One'. Heist. Marketing Services for Universities and Colleges

Pettigrew, A. M. (1985) *The Awakening Giant: Continuity and Change in ICI*, Basil Blackwood

Pettigrew, A. and Whipp, R. (1991) *Managing Change for Competitive Success*. Blackwell Business

Rankine, D. (1998) *How to Increase Your Chances of Success: A Practical Guide to Acquisitions*. Wiley/AMR

Ravenscraft, D. J. and Sherer, F. M. (1987) *Mergers, Sell-offs and Economic Efficiency*, Brookings Institute, Washington DC

Rowley, G. (1997) 'United we stand: a strategic analysis of mergers in higher education', *Public Money and Management*, October–December, 7–10

Santomero, A. M. (1999) 'Bank mergers: what's a policy maker to do?', *Journal of Banking and Finance*, Amsterdam, February, 23: 637–43

Schendel, D. (1996) The editor's introduction to the 1996 winter special issue: 'Knowledge and the firm', *Strategic Management Journal*, 17: 1–4, winter special issue

Shanley, M. T. (1994) 'Determinants and consequences of post acquisition change', in Krogh, G. v., Sinatra, A. and Singh, H. (1994) *The Management of Corporate Acquisitions*. Macmillan Press Ltd

Shelton, L. M. (1988) 'Strategic business fit and corporate acquisition: Empirical evidence', *Strategic Management Journal*, 9, 3: 279–287

Singh, H. and Montgomery, C. A. (1987) 'Corporate acquisitions and economic performance', *Strategic Management Journal*, 8: 377–386

Singh, H. and Zollo, M. (1997) 'Learning to acquire: Knowledge accumulation mechanisms and the evolution of post-acquisition integration strategies', The Wharton School, University of Pennsylvania. Working Paper 97-10-B

Slack, N., Chambers, S., Harland, C., Harrison, A. and Johnston, R. (1998) *Operations Management*. Financial Times Pitman Publishing, 2nd edn.

Szulanski, G. (1997) 'Intra-firm transfer of best practices, in Campbell, A. and Luchs, K. S. *Core-Competency Based Strategy*, International Thomson Business Press

Temple, P. and Whitchurch, C. (1994) 'An international perspective: Recent growth mergers in British Higher Education', Chapter 13 in *Merging Colleges for Mutual Growth: A New Strategy for Academic Managers*. John Hopkins University Press

Trompenaars, F. and Hampden-Turner, C. (1999) *Riding the Waves of Culture: Understanding Cultural Diversity in Business*, 2nd edn., Nicholas Brealey Publishing

Walsh, J. P. and Ellwood, J. W. (1991) 'Mergers, acquisitions and the pruning of managerial dead wood', *Strategic Management Journal*, 12: 201–17

Walter (1985) 'Cultural collisions in mergers and acquisitions', cited in Frost, P. *et al.* eds (1985) *Organisational Culture*, Sage

Wensley, R. and Angwin, D. N. (1996) 'Autonomy in post-acquisition management', Presentation at the Rembrandt Hotel, London

Wilson, D. C. (1992) *A Strategy of Change: Concepts and Controversies in the Management of Change*, Routledge

Yunker, J. A. (1983) *Integrating Acquisitions: Making Corporate Marriages Work*. Praeger

Zeldin, T. (1983) *The French*, The Harvill Press

Index